D1055821

the midst of an Age of Mary and an Age of the Holy Spirit:

> They shall be the true apostles of the latter times, to whom the Lord of Hosts shall give the words and the might to work marvels and to carry off with glory the spoils of His enemies. . . . They shall be like clouds thundering and flying through the air at the least breath of the Holy Spirit; who, detaching themselves from everything and troubling themselves about nothing, shall shower forth the rain of the Word of God and of life eternal . . . all those to whom they shall be sent on the part of the Most High.[8]

Even secular observers are beginning to sense that something special may be happening. *Commentary*, a respected intellectual journal, in order to celebrate its fiftieth year of publication (November 1995), took stock of the nation's condition. A dominant theme that emerged in the articles was the call for and recognition of perhaps the beginnings of religious revival. Various contributors suggest either that (1) the times demand another Great Awakening, or that (2) the nation is poised on the verge of a mass religious revival, or that (3) a Great Awakening is in fact already underway.

There are many prophetic confirmations of such a sense. Estela Ruiz, a respected Marian messenger, claims that Mary recently communicated to her that "there will be a great movement of souls that will come back to God this year."

[8] St. Louis de Montfort, *True Devotion to Mary*, 28–35.

Jack Hayford, a well-respected Protestant pastor, after surveying what he sees as many signs of the Spirit's working in movements of worship, intercession, reconciliation, unity, and repentance, says:

> I'm not ready to announce that this is the last move — the end-time revival — because it isn't necessary to claim it as that before we can participate in it. We are on the verge of the greatest move of God in human history! That's good enough for me.
>
> Let's all be willing to step beyond our own isolated streams of Christian experience and share in the excitement of the Holy Spirit's work in the streams of others. After all, these streams are, even now, converging into one mighty river — and the world is about to be flooded with the glory of God.[9]

These words resonate with those of John Paul II in his comparison of Christian history to streams flowing together into a single river: "The whole of Christian history appears to us as a single river, into which many tributaries pour their waters. The year 2000 invites us to gather with renewed fidelity and ever deeper communion *along the banks of this great river:* the river of Revelation, of Christianity and of the Church, a river which flows through human history. . . . This is truly the 'river' which with its 'streams,' in the expression of the Psalm, 'make glad the city of God' (46:4)."[10]

Fr. Werenfried van Straaten, who heads the Aid to the

---

[9] Jack Hayford, "Seven Signs of Imminent Grace", *Charisma Magazine* (December 1995), 69.

[10] John Paul II, *On Preparation for the Jubilee of the Year 2000*, 25.

Church in Need foundation, which gives more than seventy million dollars a year to help the Church in mainly Third World countries, is also longing for this great outpouring.

> I hope this divine intervention is imminent. Despite the menacing problems that no statesman on earth can resolve, I dare to await the worldwide outpouring of the Holy Spirit. And I believe that all the expectations that have been raised by prophets and holy mystics over thousands of years will now be realized in the fulfillment of a prophecy of Ezekiel, which is a summary of all the others.
>
> For thus says the Lord, "I will sprinkle clean water upon you and you shall be clean from all your uncleannesses, and from all your idols I will cleanse you. A new heart I will give you, and a new spirit I will put within you; and I will take out of your flesh the heart of stone and give you a heart of flesh. And I will put my spirit within you and cause you to walk in my statutes and be careful to observe my ordinances. . . . And you shall be my people and I will be your God" (Ezek 36:25–28).

While reports like these continue to multiply, some of the prophetic indications get even more specific. Let's consider some of the more notable of these.

First, we have the accounts of the vision that Pope Leo XIII is reported to have had shortly before the beginning of this century. The story has come down to us through various confidants of the Pope, primarily cardinals who were close to him.[10] While these accounts differ in exact details, the main lines of the incident are clear. While concluding a liturgical celebration in the last part of the nineteenth century in the Vatican, Leo XIII suddenly stopped and looked transfixed. He later recounted to his close collaborators what he had experienced. He had been allowed by the Lord to overhear a conversation between Satan and the Lord. The conversation was reminiscent of the conversation that Satan and the Lord had regarding the testing of Job, recounted in the Book of Job. Satan declared that if he had enough time and enough power he would be able to destroy the Church. God gave permission to Satan to take the bulk of the twentieth century as a time in which he would be allowed in a special way to test and tempt the Church, but after that his power would be limited again. It was as a result of this vision that Leo XIII asked that a special prayer to St. Michael the Archangel be said after every Mass throughout the world. This was done until about the time of the Second Vatican Council. It was also Leo XIII who asked that prayer for an outpouring of the Holy Spirit upon the Church be prayed throughout the world on the first day of the twentieth century. On this very day, in Topeka, Kansas, the Pentecostal movement was born among a group of Protestants studying the Acts of the Apostles together in a farmhouse.

Another spiritual event that sheds considerable light on the history of the twentieth century is the apparitions of Mary in Fatima, Portugal, in 1917. At that time, as World

---

[10] Stefano M. Paci, "Leo XIII's Diabolical Vision", *30 Days*, December, 1990, 52–53. See also, John J. Nicola, *Diabolical Possession and Exorcism* (Rockford, Ill.: Tan Books and Publishers, 1974), 151.

War I was still raging, the Bolshevik revolution in Russia had not yet consolidated itself; there was considerable civil war and the possibility of outside intervention. Mary prophesied in her apparitions to the children that unless there was a widespread repentance in the world and a return to the Lord, there would be another and greater world war, and Russia would spread its errors throughout the world; but in the end Russia would be converted.

Have we seen in the sudden and unexpected collapse of communism the beginnings of the fulfillment of Mary's prophetic words? Have we seen in the fall of communism and the tremendous upsurge in the preaching of the gospel in the former Soviet empire the beginnings of the end of the unusual satanic hold that has gripped the world for so many years? Are we seeing in the purification and humbling of the Church that is going on, as sin is exposed and weakness is made apparent, the preparation for a new outpouring of the Holy Spirit that will equip a humbled, purified Church to proclaim the gospel in power? Are we seeing in the extreme consequences of rebellion against God, manifesting themselves throughout the world, God's merciful judgments, which are preparing the world to listen with new ears to the good news of Jesus Christ? Are we seeing in the reports of hundreds of thousands turning to Christ in the former Soviet empire, and in the underground Church of China, or in the evangelical, Pentecostal upsurge in Latin America and Africa signs of a new age of evangelization that both Protestant and Catholic leaders have proclaimed and prophesied?

John Paul II has stated:

God is opening before the Church the horizons of a humanity more fully prepared for the sowing of the Gospel. I sense the moment has come to commit all the Church's energies to a new evangelization. . . . No believer in Christ, no institution of the Church can avoid this supreme duty: to proclaim Christ to all peoples.[11]

John Paul also clearly attributes to Mary a role in the sudden collapse of communism in 1989.

It would be difficult not to recall that the Marian Year took place only shortly before *the events of 1989*. Those events remain surprising for their vastness and especially for the speed with which they occurred. . . . In the unfolding of those events one could already discern the invisible hand of Providence at work with maternal care: "Can a woman forget her infant . . . ?" (Is 49:15).[12]

Fr. Stefano Gobbi, an Italian priest, has founded a worldwide Marian Movement of Priests, which has inspired thousands of priests and laypeople through its local units of prayer and outreach called *Cenacles* and through the annual publication of locutions Fr. Gobbi claims to be receiving from Mary. While repeating many of the themes of other Marian interventions about the urgency of the times, the reality of widespread apostasy, and the imminent victory of Christ through Mary, these locutions are also quite specific about the special significance of the

[11] John Paul II, *Mission of the Redeemer*, 3, 86.
[12] John Paul II, *On Preparation for the Jubilee of the Year 2000*, 27.

next several years. At least two of these appears to claim that Jesus is returning either in 1998 or by the year 2000.

A Period of Ten Years

Fr. Gobbi says this message was given him on September 18, 1988, at Lourdes, France. It was published in the Marian Movement of Priests' official publication of Fr. Gobbi's locutions, number 389:

These are ten very important years. These are ten decisive years. I am asking you to spend them with me because you are entering into the final period of the second Advent, which will lead you to the triumph of my Immaculate Heart in the glorious coming of my Son Jesus.

In this period of ten years there will come to completion that fullness of time which was pointed out to you by me, beginning with La Salette all the way to my most recent and present apparitions.

In this period of ten years there will come to its culmination that purification which, for a number of years now, you have been living through and therefore the sufferings will become greater for all.

In this period of ten years there will come to completion the time of the great tribulation, which has been foretold to you in Holy Scripture, before the second coming of Jesus.

In this period of ten years the mystery of iniquity, prepared for by the ever increasing spread of apostasy, will become manifest.

In this period of ten years, all the secrets which I have revealed to some of my children will come to pass and all the events which have been foretold to you by me will take place.

Later on, in December of 1994, at the Shrine of Our Lady of Guadalupe in Mexico City, Fr. Gobbi experienced a locution which set the date for the Lord's return to be by the year 2000:

I confirm to you that, by the Great Jubilee of the year 2000, there will take place the triumph of my Immaculate Heart, of which I foretold you at Fatima, and this will come to pass with the return of Jesus in glory to establish his reign in the world. Thus you will at last be able to see with your own eyes the new heaven and the new earth (Marian Movement of Priests, number 532).

What to make of all this? Let's take a look at the actual events that are unfolding and the prophetic words that accompany them in the light of what Scripture says about Jesus' return.

Is Jesus Returning Soon? Positive Indications

1. For the first time since the Jewish nation was dispersed and displaced from the land of Israel at the hands of the Romans in fulfillment of the prophecy of Jesus, the Jews have come to exist again as a nation in the Holy Land and Jerusalem is no longer trampled down by the Gentiles but

is under Israeli control. The relatively recent emergence of a small, but growing, messianic Judaism may be the first sign of something larger.

2. Much progress in world evangelization has taken place. The means now exist for the first time in history to communicate very quickly with virtually the whole world through television and radio, and significant capacities to do so are being developed by Christians. There is much prophetic indication that a great wave of world evangelization is about to break, even from those who don't necessarily connect it with the return of Jesus.

3. Something very much like a mass apostasy is taking place among the traditionally Christian nations, with vast numbers of the baptized turning away from their faith. False teachers and preachers lead many astray.

4. A manifest removal of many restraints on the working of evil and lawlessness has occurred in recent decades. As the Christian nations have "emancipated" themselves from God, lawlessness has rapidly increased.

5. There has been both a rise in the acceptance and pervasive presence of the occult, as many turn from true faith, as well as a rise in true signs and wonders and charismatic manifestations of the Spirit in the service of the gospel and the Church.

6. This upsurge in prophetic activity and the manifestation of charismatic gifts of the Spirit in both Catholic and Protestant circles is unprecedented, in my opinion, since the early days of the Church. In the Catholic Church the Marian form of a major stream of prophetic activity is also unprecedented in its frequency and extent. Much of this prophetic activity speaks of very critical years ahead

of us involving purification, tribulation, possible chastisement, as well as a great outpouring of grace and mercy on the world, ushering in either the return of Jesus himself or at least a "new springtime of Christianity".

Is Jesus Returning Soon? Cautions

1. Timing remains a mystery. For the Lord one day is as a thousand years and a thousand years are as one day. Scripture says that Jesus is coming soon. "Soon" for the Lord is obviously compatible with at least two thousand years of our human measurement of time.

2. The interpretation of prophecy remains a challenge. The prophecies concerning the coming of the Messiah in the Old Testament are much clearer in retrospect after their fulfillment than they obviously were to the Jews of the time. I suspect the same will be true of the unfulfilled prophecies in the Scriptures concerning Jesus' Second Coming in glory as well as of the contemporary prophesies concerning his return. They also will be much clearer in retrospect.

3. Because of the above, I would be very cautious in approaching messages such as those Fr. Gobbi claims to have received from Mary concerning the return of Jesus in 1998 or 2000. This seems perilously close to specifying the return of the Lord in a way that is not compatible with the spirit of Jesus' warning to the contrary and not harmonious with other messages of Mary in much more solidly attested communications. Our prophecy, like our knowledge, is currently imperfect (1 Cor 13:9), which isn't

to say that either is not valuable; valuable, just not perfect.

4. Determining what would "count" in the eyes of the Lord to fulfill the requirement that the gospel be preached to all the nations before the Lord's return is probably impossible for any human being to specify. A recurring pattern of the Lord's dealings with the human race indicates that sometimes only a relatively few can fulfill the requirements of God in such a way as to bring great blessing to many. Again, the prophecy in Scripture and in the contemporary Church gives indications that cause us to be alert and sensitive, but there is irreducible mystery as well.

5. It seems to me that, compared to the rest of Christian history, our time could be fairly described as fulfilling better than any other time the scriptural warnings about the mass apostasy and the removal of the restrainer on lawlessness. Yet, we have to remember that if the Lord does not come soon, a future time of Christian history may even better fulfill these wretched realities than we do today. God forbid!

Conclusions

The most valuable part of this book, I believe, are the chapters that outline what the Scriptures really say about the Lord's return and the events that accompany it, within the context of the basic message of salvation and redemption, and the implications for daily Christian life. And yet it is only reasonable for readers to ask, as they have done periodically over the years, what I think about these

Scriptures' applicability to our time. Let me tell you, very simply.

I think that these years we are living in are very special times in the history both of the world and of the Church. The conflict between good and evil is intensifying, in what appears to be merely human and what appears to be more than human. In my judgment the multiplicity of angel sightings is not just a new age fad. Forces are gathering; the battle is intensifying. Great mercy and grace are being offered to the human race in so many ways. And great evil is unfolding. The pressure on youth today is almost unbearable.

I think it is hard to exaggerate the significance of the activity of Mary in recent years and the reappearance on a widespread scale of the charisms of the Holy Spirit not seen in this way since the early Church. Something very special is being offered the human race: an opportunity to repent, to believe, to turn to God. An opportunity for eternal life. I think it's very possible, as St. Louis de Montfort prophesied, that the twentieth century will be known as the Age of Mary and the Age of the Holy Spirit. And just as God in his unfathomable wisdom chose Mary to prepare the Lord's First Coming, so he is sending her again to prepare for the Lord's Second Coming, using her to raise up apostles and prophets for the last days.

And yet perhaps what we are seeing unfold around us is not yet the last days in the sense of the time immediately before the Lord's return. Perhaps what we are seeing is preparation and unfolding of the end of an age: the end of seventeen hundred years of Christendom and the return of the Church to an existence like she had in the early centuries, a minority body in the midst of a pagan empire, yet full of faith, hope, and love, the gospel spreading, Christ triumphing even in the apparent defeat of his disciples. Perhaps what we are seeing is preparation, not for the final harvest, but yet for something nonetheless wonderful, a new springtime of Christianity, where currently divided Christians find themselves closer together as they witness together to him in the midst of a lawless, anti-Christian world. God again using the weak things of the world, things the world despises, to confound the wisdom of the world, so that in the days to come faith might not rest just on words or formulas but on the power of God manifested in Word and Spirit.

Is Jesus coming soon? I don't know. He very well might be; many signs point to it. But whether or not he comes in the next few years, it certainly seems as if we're in for some very special times. Chastisement, tribulation, purification, mercy, renewal, revival, repentance, new evangelization, new Pentecost, reconciliation, new springtime, are somehow, I believe, all part of the picture.

But whether or not he comes in the next few years, or even whether or not the new springtime comes, is not the most significant thing. The most significant thing is that Jesus is the same yesterday, today, and forever and that we can know and love him now and follow him, no matter what happens or doesn't happen in the world and Church around us. He surely is present now and wanting to come to each and every one of us as we open our hearts and minds to him and surrender to the grace he offers us all. He is coming. He is truly coming in so many ways to all of us. In the signs he gives us in the daily experience of our life. In his word. In "chance encounters". In his servants. In the poor, the sick, the handicapped. In the unexpected. In the neighbor of the moment. In the gentle power of the sacraments. In the cleansing of reconciliation, in the unfathomable love and intimacy of Eucharist, in the mystery and sign of marriage, in the abiding presence of orders, in the new birth of baptism and confirmation, in the comfort and healing of anointing. In our hearts always, dwelling within us, Father, Son, and Holy Spirit. Christ in us, the hope of glory, in every century, in any century, in good times and bad times, in dull times and exciting times, in times of supernatural explosion, in times when the voice of the prophet is no longer heard in the land, the amazing, inexhaustible shared love of Father, Son, and Holy Spirit. Shared with us, in us, and through us. Forever. Now.

Truly, truly: Come, Lord Jesus, come.

Selections from
St. Athanasius

St. Athanasius was born in Egypt in about A.D. 298. He was alive, then, during the last and greatest of the persecutions of Christians, after forty years of peace, which took place between the years 303 and 311. This persecution, first of Diocletian and then of Maximin, was particularly strong in Egypt, and Athanasius witnessed at first hand the courage of Christian martyrs. He was elected bishop of Alexandria in 328, and the great thrust of his life was the defense of the fundamental Christian truths — especially regarding the Incarnation and redemption — that were severely attacked in the Arian reaction after the Council of Nicaea in 325. He suffered for his defense of the faith and was exiled five times from his responsibilities as bishop, dying finally in 373. I have chosen here some selections from his work *On the Incarnation* for several rea-

The Appendix is excerpted from *St. Athanasius on the Incarnation* (Crestwood, N.Y.: St. Vladimir's Seminary Press, 1953. Used with permission of A. R. Mowbray's, Oxford, England, owners of the rights to the English translation.

sons. The selections give a remarkably vivid picture of the dynamic orthodoxy of the Catholic Church of that time and of the vital interplay of the institutional, charismatic, and missionary dimensions of the Church. These selections also give an inspiring picture of orthodox, Christ-centered, Spirit-filled Church life and evangelistic activity that can very well serve as an inspiration for the "new evangelization" that John Paul II has constantly called for and as an inspiring picture of what the "new springtime of Christianity" may indeed look like as it unfolds. The readings also provide a key to the success of this dynamic life and mission in their unambiguous focus on the person of Christ, his death, Resurrection, and return in glory, and on the wholehearted surrender and commitment he deserves, which bears much fruit in the life of his disciples and in the spread of the gospel.

The Depth of the Fall

§5 This, then, was the plight of men. God had not only made them out of nothing, but had also graciously bestowed on them His own life by the grace of the Word. Then, turning from eternal things to things corruptible, by counsel of the devil, they had become the cause of their own corruption in death; for, as I said before, though they were by nature subject to corruption, the grace of their union with the Word made them capable of escaping from the natural law, provided that they retained the beauty of innocence with which they were created. That is to say, the presence of the Word with them shielded them even from natural corruption, as also Wisdom says: "God created man for incorruption and as an image of His own eternity; but by envy of the devil death entered into the world" (Wis 2:23f.). When this happened, men began to die, and corruption ran riot among them and held sway over them to an even more than natural degree, because it was the penalty of which God had forewarned them for transgressing the commandment. Indeed, they had in their sinning surpassed all limits; for, having invented wickedness in the beginning and so involved themselves in death and corruption, they had gone on gradually from bad to worse, not stopping at any one kind of evil, but continually, as with insatiable appetite, devising new kinds of sins.

§12 Yet men, bowed down by the pleasures of the moment and by the frauds and illusions of the evil spirits, did not lift up their heads towards the truth. So burdened were they with their wickednesses that they seemed rather to be brute beasts than reasonable men, reflecting the very Likeness of the Word.

§6 . . . Because death and corruption were gaining ever firmer hold on them, the human race was in process of destruction. Man, who was created in God's image and in his possession of reason reflected the very Word Himself, was disappearing, and the work of God was being undone. The law of death, which followed from the Transgression, prevailed upon us, and from it there was no escape. The thing that was happening was in truth both monstrous and unfitting. It would, of course, have been unthinkable that God should go back upon His word and that man, having transgressed, should not die; but it was equally monstrous that beings which once had shared the nature of the Word should perish and turn back again into non-existence through corruption. It was unworthy of the goodness of God that creatures made by Him should be brought to nothing through the deceit wrought upon man by the devil; and it was supremely unfitting that the work of God in mankind should disappear, either through their own negligence or through the deceit of evil spirits. As, then, the creatures whom He had created reasonable, like the Word, were in fact perishing, and such noble works were on the road to ruin, what then was God, being Good, to do?

The Need for Redemption

§7 Was He to demand repentance from men for their transgression? You might say that that was worthy of God, and argue further that, as through the Transgression they became subject to corruption, so through repentance they might return to incorruption again. But repentance would not guard the Divine consistency, for, if death did not hold dominion over men, God would still remain untrue. Nor does repentance recall men from what is according to their nature; all that it does is make them cease from sinning. Had it been a case of a trespass only, and not of a subsequent corruption, repentance would have been well enough; but when once transgression had begun men came under the power of the corruption proper to their nature and were bereft of the grace which belonged to them as creatures in the Image of God. No, repentance could not meet the case. What—or rather *Who* was it that was needed for such grace and such recall as we required? Who, save the Word of God Himself, Who also in the beginning had made all things out of nothing? His part it was, and His alone, both to bring again the corruptible to incorruption and to maintain for the Father His consistency of character with all. For He alone, being Word of the Father and above all, was in consequence both able to recreate all, and worthy to suffer on behalf of all and to be an ambassador for all with the Father.

§8 He saw the reasonable race, the race of men that, like Himself, expressed the Father's Mind, wasting out of existence, and death reigning over all in corruption. He saw that corruption held us all the closer, because it was the penalty for the Transgression; He saw, too, how unthinkable it would be for the law to be repealed before it was fulfilled. He saw how unseemly it was that the very things of which He Himself was the Artificer should be disappearing. He saw how the surpassing wickedness of men was mounting up against them; He saw also their universal liability to death. All this He saw and, pitying our race, moved with compassion for our limitation, unable to endure that death should have the mastery, rather than that His creatures should perish and the work of His Father for us men come to nought, He took to Himself a body, a human body even as our own.

§8 Thus, taking a body like our own, because all our bodies were liable to the corruption of death, He surrendered His body to death in place of all, and offered it to the Father. This He did out of sheer love for us, so that in His death all might die, and the law of death thereby be abolished because, when He had fulfilled in His body that for which it was appointed, it was thereafter voided of its power for men. This He did that He might turn again to incorruption men who had turned back to corruption, and make them alive through death by the appropriation of His body and by the grace of His resurrection. Thus He would make death to disappear from them as utterly as straw from fire.

§9 The Word perceived that corruption could not be got rid of otherwise than through death; yet He Himself, as the Word, being immortal and the Father's Son, was such as could not die. For this reason, therefore, He assumed a body capable of death, in order that it, through belonging to the Word Who is above all, might become in dying a sufficient exchange for all, and, itself remaining incorruptible through His indwelling, might thereafter put an end to corruption for all others as well, by grace of the resurrection. It was by surrendering to death the body which He had taken, as an offering and sacrifice free from every stain, that He forthwith abolished death for His human brethren by the offering of the equivalent. For naturally, since the Word of God was above all, when He offered

His own temple and bodily instrument as a substitute for the life of all, He fulfilled in death all that was required.

§14 When the madness of idolatry and irreligion filled the world and the knowledge of God was hidden, whose part was it to teach the world about the Father? Man's, would you say? But men cannot run everywhere over the world, nor would their words carry sufficient weight if they did, nor would they be unaided, a match for the evil spirits. Moreover, since even the best of men were confused and blinded by evil, how could they convert the souls and minds of others? You cannot put straight in others what is warped in yourself. Perhaps you will say, then, that creation was enough to teach men about the Father. But if that had been so, such great evils would never had occurred. Creation was there all the time, but it did not prevent men from wallowing in error. Once more, then, it was the Word of God, Who sees all that is in man and moves all things in creation, Who alone could meet the needs of the situation.

§20 But beyond all this, there was a debt owing which must needs be paid; for, as I said before, all men were due to die. Here, then, is the second reason why the Word dwelt among us, namely, that having proved His Godhead by His works, He might offer the sacrifice on behalf of all, surrendering His own temple to death in place of all, to settle man's account with death and free him from the primal transgression.

Death there had to be, and death for all, so that the due of all might be paid. Wherefore, the Word, as I said, being

Himself incapable of death, assumed a mortal body, that He might offer it as His own in place of all, and suffering for the sake of all through His union with it, "might bring to nought Him that had the power of death, that is, the devil, and might deliver them who all their lifetime were enslaved by the fear of death" (Heb 2:14f.).

§25 But if any honest Christian wants to know why He suffered death on the cross and not in some other way, we answer thus: in no other way was it expedient for us, indeed the Lord offered for our sakes the one death that was supremely good. He had come to bear the curse that lay on us; and how could He "become a curse" (Gal 3:13) otherwise than by accepting the accursed death? And that death is the cross, for it is written "Cursed is every one that hangeth on a tree" (Gal 3:13).

The Fruits of Redemption

§10 For by the sacrifice of His own body He did two things: He put an end to the law of death which barred our way; and He made a new beginning of life for us, by giving us the hope of resurrection.

Now, therefore, when we die we no longer do so as men condemned to death, but as those who are even now in process of rising we await the general resurrection of all, "which in its own times He shall show" (1 Tim 6:15), even God Who wrought it and bestowed it on us.

§21 Have no fear, then. Now that the common Saviour of all has died on our behalf, we who believe in Christ no longer die, as men died aforetime, in fulfillment of the threat of the law. That condemnation has come to an end; and now that, by the grace of the resurrection, corruption has been banished and done away [with], we are loosed from our mortal bodies in God's good time for each, so that we may obtain thereby a better resurrection. Like seeds cast into the earth, we do not perish in our dissolution, but like them shall rise again, death having been brought to nought by the grace of the Saviour.

§22 The supreme object of His coming was to bring about the resurrection of the body. This was to be the monument to His victory over death, the assurance to all that He had Himself conquered corruption and that their own bodies also would eventually be incorrupt; and it was in token of that and as a pledge of the future resurrection that He kept His body incorrupt.

The Witness of Christ and of Christians

§27 A very strong proof of this destruction of death and its conquest by the cross is supplied by a present fact, namely this. All the disciples of Christ despise death; they take the offensive against it and, instead of fearing it, by the sign of the cross and by faith in Christ trample on it as on something dead. Before the divine advent of the Saviour even the holiest of men were afraid of death, and mourned the dead as those who perish. But now that the Saviour has raised His body, death is no longer terrible, but all those who believe in Christ tread it under-

foot as nothing, and prefer to die rather than to deny
their faith in Christ, knowing full well that when they
die they do not perish, but live indeed, and become incorruptible through the resurrection. But that devil who
of old wickedly exulted in death, now that the pains of
death are loosed, he alone it is who remains truly dead.
There is proof of this too; for men who, before they believe in Christ, think death horrible and are afraid of it,
once they are converted despise it so completely that they
go eagerly to meet it, and themselves become witnesses of
the Saviour's resurrection from it. Even children hasten
thus to die, and not men only, but women train themselves by bodily discipline to meet it. So weak has death
become that even women, who used to be taken in by it,
mock at it now as a dead thing robbed of all its strength.
Death has become like a tyrant who has been completely
conquered by the legitimate monarch; bound hand and
foot as he now is, the passers-by jeer at him, hitting him
and abusing him, no longer afraid of his cruelty and rage,
because of the king who has conquered him. So has death
been conquered and branded for what it is by the Saviour
on the cross. It is bound hand and foot, all who are in
Christ trample it as they pass and as witnesses to Him de-
ride it, scoffing and saying, "O Death, where is thy victory? O Grave, where is thy sting?" (1 Cor 15:55).

§28 Is this a slender proof of the impotence of death,
do you think? Or is it a slight indication of the Saviour's
victory over it, when boys and young girls who are in
Christ look beyond this present life and train themselves
to die? Every one is by nature afraid of death and of bod-

ily dissolution; the marvel of marvels is that he who is enfolded in the faith of the cross despises this natural fear and for the sake of the cross is no longer cowardly in face of it.

Even so, if anyone still doubts the conquest of death, after so many proofs and so many martyrdoms in Christ and such daily scorn of death by His truest servants, he certainly does well to marvel at so great a thing, but he must not be obstinate in unbelief and disregard of plain facts. No, he must be like the man who wants to prove the property of the asbestos, and like him who enters the conqueror's dominions to see the tyrant bound. He must embrace the faith of Christ, this disbeliever in the conquest of death, and come to His teaching. Then he will see how impotent death is and how completely conquered. Indeed, there have been many former unbelievers and deriders who, after they became believers, so scorned death as even themselves to become martyrs for Christ's sake.

§29 If, then, it is by the sign of the cross and by faith in Christ that death is trampled underfoot, it is clear that it is Christ Himself and none other Who is the Archvictor over death and has robbed it of its power. Death used to be strong and terrible, but now, since the advent of the Saviour and the death and resurrection of His body, it is despised; and obviously it is by the very Christ Who mounted on the cross that it has been destroyed and vanquished finally. When the sun rises after the night and the whole world is lit up by it, nobody doubts that it is the sun which has thus shed its light everywhere and driven away the dark. Equally clear is it, since this utter scorning and trampling down of death has ensued upon the Saviour's manifestation in the body and His death on the cross, that it is He Himself Who brought death to nought and daily raises monuments to His victory in His own disciples. How can you think otherwise, when you see men naturally weak hastening to death, unafraid at the prospect of corruption, fearless of the descent into Hades, even indeed with eager soul provoking it, not shrinking from tortures, but preferring thus to rush on death for Christ's sake, rather than to remain in this present life? If you see with your own eyes men and women and children, even, thus welcoming death for the sake of Christ's religion, how can you be so utterly silly and incredulous and maimed in your mind as not to realize that Christ, to Whom these all bear witness, Himself gives the victory to each, making death completely powerless for those who hold His faith and bear the sign of the cross? No one in his senses doubts that a snake is dead when he sees it trampled underfoot, especially when he knows how savage it used to be; nor, if he sees boys making fun of a lion, does he doubt that the brute is either dead or completely bereft of strength. These things can be seen with our own eyes, and it is the same with the conquest of death. Doubt no longer, then, when you see death mocked and scorned by those who believe in Christ, that by Christ death was destroyed, and the corruption that goes with it resolved and brought to end.

§30 The Saviour is working mightily among men; every day He is invisibly persuading numbers of people all over the world, both within and beyond the Greek-speaking world, to accept His faith and be obedient to His teaching. Can anyone, in face of this, still doubt that He has risen and can prick the consciences of men, so that they throw all the traditions of their fathers to the winds and bow down before the teachings of Christ? If He is no longer active in the world, as He must needs be if He is dead, how is it that He makes the living to cease from their activities, the adulterer from his adultery, the murderer from murdering, the unjust from avarice, while the profane and godless man becomes religious? If He did not rise, but is still dead, how is it that He routs and persecutes and overthrows the false gods, whom unbelievers think to be alive, and the evil spirits whom they worship? For where Christ is named, idolatry is destroyed and the fraud of evil spirits is exposed; indeed, no such spirit can endure that Name, but takes to flight on sound of it. This is the work of One Who lives, not of one dead; and, more than that, it is the work of God.

§31 In a word, then, those who disbelieve in the resurrection have no support in facts, if their gods and evil spirits do not drive away the supposedly dead Christ. Rather, it is He Who convicts them of being dead. We are agreed that a dead person can do nothing: yet the Saviour works mightily every day, drawing men to religion, persuading them to virtue, teaching them about immortality, quickening their thirst for heavenly things, revealing the knowledge of the Father, inspiring strength in face of death, manifesting Himself to each, and displacing the irreligion of idols; while the gods and evil spirits of the unbelievers can do none of these things, but rather become dead at

Christ's presence, all their ostentation barren and void. By the sign of the cross, on the contrary, all magic is stayed, all sorcery confounded, all the idols are abandoned and deserted, and all senseless pleasure ceases, as the eye of faith looks up from earth to heaven.

§32　It is, indeed, in accordance with the nature of the invisible God that He should be thus known through His works; and those who doubt the Lord's resurrection because they do not now behold Him with their eyes, might as well deny the very laws of nature. They have ground for disbelief when works are lacking, but when the works cry out and prove the fact so clearly, why do they deliberately deny the risen life so manifestly shown? Even if their mental faculties are defective, surely their eyes can give them irrefragable proof of the power and Godhead of Christ. A blind man cannot see the sun, but he knows that it is above the earth from the warmth which it affords; similarly, let those who are still in the blindness of unbelief recognize the Godhead of Christ and the resurrection which He has brought about through His manifested power in others. Obviously He would not be expelling evil spirits and despoiling idols, if He were dead, for the evil spirits would not obey one who was dead. If, on the other hand, the very naming of Him drives them forth, He clearly is not dead; and the more so that the spirits, who perceive things unseen by men, would know if He were so and would refuse to obey Him. But, as a matter of fact, what profane persons doubt, the evil spirits *know*—namely that He is God. And for that reason they flee from Him and fall at His feet, crying out even

Is Jesus Coming Soon?

RALPH MARTIN

Is Jesus Coming Soon?

*A Catholic Perspective
on the Second Coming*

IGNATIUS PRESS   SAN FRANCISCO

Original edition: *The Return of the Lord*
© 1983, Ralph Martin
Servant Books, Ann Arbor

Cover by Roxanne Mei Lum

Cover art: Raphael, *La Disputa*, 1509
The Debate over the Blessed Sacrament
Stanza della Segnatura
Vatican Palace, Vatican State
Erich Lessing/Art Resource, New York

© 1997 Ralph Martin
All rights reserved
ISBN 0–89870–635–1
Library of Congress catalogue number 97–70804
Printed in the United States of America ⊗

Contents

Introduction

The core of this book was first published in 1983 and was well received at that time. It is now being published in a revised version with an additional chapter that attempts to provide an orientation to the explosion of the supernatural that seems to be taking place as we approach the new millennium. Why this book? Why now?

Each year as the Advent season approaches and we begin to hear the striking readings concerning the destruction of Jerusalem and the Second Coming of Jesus, I long to hear something about these "final things", but more often than not I do not. Despite the centrality of the Second Coming to the Catholic faith, despite how deeply embedded it is in Scripture, doctrine, and liturgy, Catholics by and large are amazingly ignorant about this important reality, this completion of the basic gospel message. Very seldom is this reality taught or preached clearly in all its richness and all its glorious implications. Very seldom does this foundational truth function as a daily source of comfort, encouragement, and vigilance as the Scriptures clearly indicate it should. Thus, this book.

Another reason why it is important for Catholics (and all Christians, of course) to be clear on the scriptural teaching concerning the Second Coming, as it has been understood in the life of the Church over the centuries, is that there is clearly an acceleration of the supernatural

7

in our time, whether it be by Marian apparitions or Pentecostal prophecy that often speaks of impending events that are sometimes interpreted as preludes to the Lord's return. Discernment is necessary. Prophecy should not be despised but should be tested. The Spirit is speaking to the Church as she approaches the birth of a new millennium, but discernment and testing are necessary if we are not to be misled or develop a Christian life that is imbalanced. An important base for this discernment is knowledge of what Scripture itself says about the "end times" and the events that must transpire before the Lord returns, as well as about what our attitude and actions should be in response to these events. Thus, this book.

The next several years promise to be full of opportunity and conflict as the world and Church move toward what some speak of as the possible birth of a new age. John Paul II has spoken of a veritable "new springtime" for Christianity and claims already to be able to see its first signs. Hopefully this book may make a small contribution to our having that "enlightened" zeal that the apostle Paul speaks about as we wait and work for both this "new springtime" and, even more, the Lord's return.

ONE

Basic Questions: The Fate of Man, the Life of God

Before we turn specifically to the issues concerning the Second Coming, it is important, in these early chapters, to establish the framework in which it functions, namely, the final stage of the plan of salvation, the final good news of the basic gospel message. What is this plan of salvation? What is this message of good news, of which the Second Coming forms the final part? Let's begin by considering the basic situation in which we human beings find ourselves.

Most of us go about our daily routines untroubled by the basic questions of life. But sometimes those questions break through, and we realize that we are living in a culture that shields us from some of the fundamental realities underlying the human condition.

Our attention is drawn to the "beautiful people" as they earn lots of money, marry their third spouses, make brilliant scientific discoveries, break sports records, model new clothes, travel to Paris, win an election, have babies, get promotions. Not nearly so much attention is paid to the "beautiful people" as they get old and die, their bodies full of cancer, their hearts diseased, their livers, kidneys, and brains degenerating; their relationships often broken and strewn with deceit, treachery, hatred, and resentment; their last days spent in a mist of alcohol and drugs, an attempt to block out the unpleasant realities of life.

And what of the "unbeautiful people" — the billions of uneducated, unaffluent human beings who *don't* break sports records, wear the latest fashions, attend the opera or theater, go to school, travel to Paris, or buy books? The underlying misery of the human condition is closer to them and less hidden; they have fewer "advances" in civilization to hide or mask it. They fight off rats, steal for food, have their energy sapped by intestinal parasites. The dead bodies of their children and parents lie briefly in the rooms of their huts and flats, unembalmed, covered with flies, quickly buried.

Disguised for the first group, stark for the second, their end is identical and common to all men: humiliation in death. Rich or poor, white or black, peasant or city dweller, educated or uneducated, beautiful or unbeautiful — all meet the same fate. When the noise that distracts us finally quiets, when the entertainments that anesthetize us finally end, in an anxious moment of a sleepless night, the words of the psalmist speak the dreaded truth: "What is man, that you notice him; the son of man, that you take thought of him? Man is like a breath; his days, like a passing shadow" (Ps 144:3–4).

And the life of God? He is without end or beginning, an eternal and infinite communion of love, three Persons, profoundly one. All that exists — the entire universe, seen and unseen, discovered, yet to be discovered, and perhaps never to be discovered — is but an image of his glory.

God: Father, Son, and Holy Spirit. A life vastly greater than the space covered by galaxies speeding away from each other from the beginning of the universe until the end of time. A life of greater power than the simultaneous conversion of all the matter in the universe into energy — more power than exploding supernova a billion billion times over. A life of infinitely more beauty than the most exquisite flowers, sunsets, musical compositions, paintings, dances, and mathematical theorems; of infinitely more truth than all that mankind knows or will ever know. A life of greater love and mercy, tenderness and goodness; of greater joy and delight, happiness and bliss than it has ever entered into the heart of man even to imagine. A life of abundance, freedom, and majesty, of profound and enduring greatness, that causes us — in the still moment of knowing God, glimpsed momentarily in his creation — to say, whisper, shout, with the psalmist:

> The heavens declare the glory of God,
>   and the firmament proclaims his handiwork.
> Day pours out the word to day,
>   and night to night imparts knowledge;
> not a word nor a discourse
>   whose voice is not heard;
> Through all the earth their voice resounds,
>   and to the ends of the world, their message. . . .

O Lord, our Lord,
how glorious is your name over all the earth!

(Ps 19:1–5; 8:10)

How did man come to such a miserable condition when he was created by such a magnificent God? Is it possible for man to be rescued from his wretched end? If so, how? These are the basic questions.

TWO

In the Beginning

In the beginning was God — simply, totally, magnificently, stupendously. He needed and wanted nothing. He was eternally full and complete, living, loving, knowing, and being, with a majesty, perfection, and glory beyond the languages of men.

Out of this fullness of life and love, God the Father brought forth the universe through, with, and in his only begotten Son, in the power of the Holy Spirit. God decided there would be something rather than nothing; so he created the universe, giving it a structure and life that in some dim but real way reflected his own. In the midst of the vastness of the universe, he created the conditions that led to the existence of the planet that is our home: earth, third planet of the star we call the sun, one among one hundred billion other stars in the galaxy we call the Milky Way, in a family of galaxies expanding and speeding away from earth.

On this planet God created all forms of life. As his culminating achievement, he fashioned man in his own image and likeness. Out of his extraordinary love, profound wisdom, and indescribable goodness, God created a race like himself—able in some way to know and love, choose and decide, think and speak, build and destroy. They were limited creatures, certainly, but had a potential to share something of the infinite depth and vitality of the life of God.

Of all the wondrous endowments God granted the human race, perhaps the most extraordinary was that of genuine freedom. For man was created perfectly free, able even to accept or reject his Creator. The choice was man's: either to take part in God's plan for the universe and the human race or to refuse this cooperation, to rebel.

I remember when, as a boy, I first began to perceive the greatness and identity of God and our utter dependence on him. At the time it seemed to me inconceivable that anyone would ever reject God or that God might allow such a thing. Then, as I saw that God allowed this terrifying alternative and that many men chose it, my incredulity yielded to horror—for I too was a man. I began to pray that God would take away my awful freedom and oblige me to obey him. Of course, God did not do that. As I grew older I too had to sort out the voices that invite a man to enlist his freedom in their causes. I too came to experience in my own life the conflict of sin and grace, rebellion and obedience, which makes up the heart of the story of our race.

Just as it is painful for men to be led from a dark room into bright sunlight, so too it is painful for fallen human beings to be confronted with the brightness of God and his Word. Our timid, fearful, proud, rebellious minds recoil as God's truth and Word are revealed to us. We undergo the pain of readjustment, submission, and change as we move from our narrow, dark, and human world, with its man-size thoughts and truths, into the realm of the divine.

In those first years of spiritual awareness, my mind reeled before the reality of human freedom in the face of God. Later, I was dumbfounded at a glimpse of God's eternity, shocked before the reality of the Incarnation, awestruck at the identity of the Crucified One, and stupefied by and scarcely daring to believe the extraordinary invitation of the resurrected Christ.

But I might have expected as much, and so might you. If God is truly God and man is truly man, their ways of viewing, evaluating, and ordering things should be considerably different. This may be elementary, yet sometimes it has taken prophets like Isaiah to remind us of this simple, world-shattering difference:

> For my thoughts are not your thoughts,
>   nor are your ways my ways, says the Lord.
> As high as the heavens are above the earth,
>   so high are my ways above your ways
>   and my thoughts above your thoughts.

> (Is 55:8–9)

Experiences of great suffering and pain can bring us to the point of silence in which the noise and arrogance of our thoughts subside. Then, like Job, we can be still and know that he is God and we are man, his creature.

I know that you can do all things,
  and that no purpose of yours can be hindered.
I have dealt with great things that I do not
    understand;
  things too wonderful for me, which I cannot know.
I had heard of you by word of mouth,
  but now my eye has seen you.
Therefore I disown what I have said,
  and repent in dust and ashes.

(Job 42:2–6)

An ability to listen means an ability to learn. And by listening to God's voice, we can learn the one thing necessary: his way and will, his purpose in creating us, his word about our tragic state, his provision for rescue.

The first of these free creatures were friends of God, rulers over the creation. Free, that is, until the entry of the "prince of this world" (Jn 16:11), who prompted them to rebellion, the serpent "most cunning" (Gen 3:1), he whom Jesus identified later as "a liar and murderer from the beginning" (Jn 8:44).

This first and fateful encounter reveals a great deal about Satan's tactics in leading human beings away from God. Satan begins by asking the woman a question that confuses her about the actual content of God's word: "Did God really tell you not to eat from any of the trees in the garden?" The woman tries to restate accurately what God has said but — perhaps yielding to the pressure of the question — adds a prohibition to God's command: "We may eat of the fruit of the trees in the garden; it is only about the fruit of the tree in the middle of the garden that God said, 'You shall not eat it *or even touch it,* lest you die' " (emphasis added). Having planted a seed of doubt by this initial question, Satan goes on to contradict directly what God has said; he implies that God is lying to the first humans in order to protect his own position and to keep them from a power and knowledge that is rightfully theirs. "You certainly will not die! No, God knows well that the moment you eat of it you will be like gods who know what is good and what is bad." The woman then yields to the threefold appeal of the forbidden fruit. "The woman saw that the tree was good for food, pleasing to the eyes, and desirable for gaining wisdom. So she took some of its fruit and ate it; and she also gave some to her husband, who was with her, and he ate it" (Gen 3:1–6).

This same pattern of temptation figures elsewhere — in the account of Jesus' meeting with Satan in the wilderness, for example (Mt 4:1–11). First, Satan attempts to sow doubt; then, he directly contradicts God's word and appeals to certain human desires — coveting with the eyes, wanting to be powerful, wise, and independent. Identifying this strategy of Satan became a regular element of Christian teaching:

> If anyone loves the world,
> the Father's love has no place in him,
> for nothing that the world affords
> comes from the Father.
> Carnal allurements,
> enticements for the eye,
> the life of empty show —

all these are from the world.
And the world with its seductions is passing away
but the man who does God's will
endures forever.

(1 Jn 2:15–17)

The first humans fell prey to Satan's arousal of their desires. They ate of the fruit, but then "the eyes of both of them were opened, and they realized that they were naked. . . . [T]he man and his wife hid themselves from the Lord God among the trees of the garden" (Gen 3:7, 8).

When God questions them about their disobedience, the man blames the woman, and the woman blames Satan. God holds them all responsible, however, and assigns to each the consequences of his action. God pledges hostility between the offspring of the serpent and the offspring of the woman and hints of the serpent's defeat. (In this, the early Church saw the first promise of the coming victory over Satan by *the* offspring of the woman — Jesus.)

For the woman, the specific consequences of her rebellion are that childbirth will be difficult and that she will continue to desire her husband, who will now tend to dominate her and abuse his position of authority established by God in the order of creation.

Because of the sin of the man, creation itself will be cursed. The ground will still yield food, but only at the price of exhausting labor "until you return to the ground, from which you were taken; for you are dirt, and to dirt you shall return" (Gen 3:19).

God banishes the first man and woman from the garden because of their sin. This punishment ensures that they will not eat from the tree of life and thereby live forever. He had warned them: "The moment you eat from it you are surely doomed to die" (Gen 2:17).

The Book of Wisdom sums up the tragedy in a particularly striking way:

God did not make death,
  nor does he rejoice in the destruction of the
    living. . . .
For God formed man to be imperishable;
  the image of his own nature he made him.
But by the envy of the devil, death entered the world,
  and they who are in his possession experience it.

(Wis 1:13; 2:23–24)

Who is this serpent who plays such a critical role?

The Old Testament provides glimpses of a whole order of creation distinct from men: spiritual beings who abide with God and help carry out his work. The service of these great angelic hosts occasionally calls them to break in on the world of men.

The Old Testament and — more clearly — the New Testament also describe quite another kind of spiritual being — demons. These are opposed to God and his work and actively seek to hinder it. They are led by God's spiritual archenemy, Satan, whose rebellion the Church Fathers saw described in the following account of the fall of Lucifer, the "Morning Star":

How have you fallen from the heavens,
  O morning star, son of the dawn!

How are you cut down to the ground,
  you who mowed down the nations!
You said in your heart:
  "I will scale the heavens;
Above the stars of God
  I will set up my throne;
I will take my seat on the Mount of Assembly,
  in the recesses of the North.
I will ascend above the tops of the clouds;
  I will be like the Most High!"
Yet down to the nether world you go
  to the recesses of the pit!

                         (Is 14:12–15)

The Book of Revelation offers another account of the spiritual conflict between God and Satan. After a description of the woman "clothed with the sun" who gives birth to a son, "a boy destined to rule all the nations with an iron rod", comes an account of the outbreak of war in heaven:

> Then war broke out in heaven; Michael and his angels battled against the dragon. Although the dragon and his angels fought back, they were overpowered and lost their place in heaven. The huge dragon, the ancient serpent known as the devil or Satan, the seducer of the whole world, was driven out; he was hurled down to earth and his minions with him. . . .

> "But woe to you, earth and sea,
>   for the devil has come down upon you!

His fury knows no limits,
for he knows his time is short."

When the dragon saw that he had been cast down
to earth, he pursued the woman who had given birth
to the boy (Rev 12:7–13).

Tradition has it that the rebellion of Lucifer and his
angels was occasioned by the revelation of God's plan
for the Incarnation, the identification of pure spirit with
mere flesh. His rebellion and hostility then became di-
rected to God and to God's plan to ennoble the human
race through the Incarnation.

Condemned by their rebellion to a life of hard labor and
oppressive relationships, and ultimately to death, the first
man and woman leave paradise to take up their life of exile on a cursed earth. Their minds and hearts perverted
and twisted by their new and diabolical "knowledge of
good and evil", they increase and multiply, bringing others into the world that they have caused to be fallen. Again
and again, they see the hellish quality of their sin repro-
duced in their offspring. Having rejected God and his merciful rule, the first man and woman are subjected to the
fiendish rule of the one whom they obeyed: "The whole
world is in the power of the evil one" (1 Jn 5:19). Their
God-reflecting natures deeply wounded, they fall captive
to their lusts. Life becomes a living hell, and death relent-
lessly claims its victims. Having thrown off the rule of
God, the human race now begins to devour itself, man
turning against man. Cain kills Abel out of resentment

and envy, and the story of human treachery, misery, and
evil continues unbroken until the time of Noah.

> When the Lord saw how great was man's wicked-
> ness on earth, and how no desire that his heart con-
> ceived was ever anything but evil, he regretted that
> he had made man on the earth, and his heart was
> grieved. . . . But Noah found favor with the Lord. . . .
> In the eyes of God the earth was corrupt and full of
> lawlessness (Gen 6:5–6, 8, 11).

The great flood brought God's judgment upon the
earth, but Noah — along with his companions on the ark
— was spared because of his righteousness. God then at-
tempted to reestablish the human race. He made a covenant with Noah and his family, those with him, and
through them all men. God set the rainbow in the sky
as the sign and reminder of this agreement.

But once again the plan failed. After the flood, Noah
himself sinned; and instead of providing a new start for
the human race, his descendants grew increasingly wicked.
One day they decided to collaborate in the building of a
great city and a tower, intending to display the greatness of
man, apart from God and in opposition to his will. "Then
they said, 'Come, let us build ourselves a city and a tower
with its top in the sky, and so make a name for ourselves;
otherwise we shall be scattered all over the earth' " (Gen
11:4).

God saw the defiance in these people's hearts and understood the intentions behind their building. He therefore confused their language and scattered them over the
earth.

"If now, while they are one people, all speaking the same language, they have started to do this, nothing will later stop them from doing whatever they presume to do. Let us then go down and there confuse their language, so that one will not understand what another says." Thus the Lord scattered them from there all over the earth, and they stopped building the city. That is why it was called Babel, because there the Lord confused the speech of all the world. It was from that place that he scattered them all over the earth (Gen 11:6–9).

To this day, we all suffer from this dispersion and inability to understand each other.

THREE

God Chooses a People

Although God's plan for Noah and his descendants had been frustrated, his commitment to save and reestablish the human race was enduring. This time, though, instead of attempting to renew all mankind at once, God chose to build himself a nation that would live according to his will and eventually bring the other nations to himself.

So he called and began to reveal himself to Abraham, father of the Jewish people and, indeed, of all who have faith in God. Once again, God extended his covenant love and loyalty; he promised to make Abraham father of a great nation with a land of its own and to bring blessing to the whole earth through him and his descendants. The sign of this covenant was to be marked forever in the flesh of Abraham's male descendants through circumcision.

The story of Sodom and Gomorrah reveals something of how God might have desired to use Israel as a saving people for the rest of the earth.

God reveals to Abraham that he is about to destroy Sodom and Gomorrah because "their sin [is] so grave" (Gen 18:20). Abraham intercedes for the cities, asking that they be spared for the sake of the righteous who live within them. Finally, the Lord agrees to be merciful on condition that he find ten righteous people in Sodom. Abraham's nephew, Lot, lives in that city and gives a gracious welcome to God's messengers, two angels who appear as distinguished-looking men. But Lot's fellow citizens are not so hospitable.

> Before they went to bed all the townsmen of Sodom, both young and old—all the people to the last man —closed in on the house. They called to Lot and said to him, "Where are the men who came to your house tonight? Bring them out to us so that we may have intimacies with them" (Gen 19:4–5).

This attempt to abuse the angels homosexually seals the cities' fate. Lot is warned of the impending destruction and tries to persuade his family to flee: " 'Get up and leave this place' he told them; 'the Lord is about to destroy the city.' But his sons-in-law thought he was joking" (Gen 19:14). Finally only Lot and his two unmarried daughters follow the angels' instructions and are spared.

> Early the next morning Abraham went to the place where he had stood in the Lord's presence. As he looked down towards Sodom and Gomorrah and the whole region of the Plain, he saw dense smoke over the land rising like fumes from a furnace.
> Thus it came to pass: when God destroyed the Cities of the Plain, he was mindful of Abraham by sending Lot away from the upheaval by which God overthrew the cities where Lot had been living (Gen 19:27–29).

God blessed Abraham and honored his covenant relationship with him, but he also required that Abraham fulfill his own part of the commitment. As a test of his servant's obedience, God even requested the ultimate sacrifice: Abraham's only son, Isaac, whose birth had been a great gift and a sign of God's faithfulness. Isaac was, to all appearances, the only means by which God's promises to Abraham could be fulfilled. Nowhere is Abraham's extraordinary position in salvation history more strikingly revealed than in his response to this seemingly impossible and contradictory command of the Lord. (Later, of course, God himself was to provide an even more extraordinary, seemingly impossible, and contradictory sign of his commitment to Abraham and his descendants.)

> Then God said: "Take your son Isaac, your only one, whom you love, and go to the land of Moriah. There you shall offer him up as a holocaust. . . ."
> On the third day Abraham got sight of the place from afar. . . . [He] took the wood for the holocaust and laid it on his son Isaac's shoulders, while he himself carried the fire and the knife. As the two walked on together, Isaac spoke to his father Abraham: "Father!" he said. "Yes, son," he replied. . . . "Here are the fire and the wood, but where is the sheep for the holocaust?" "Son," Abraham answered, "God himself will provide the sheep for the holocaust" (Gen 22:2, 4, 6–8).

Two thousand years later God did provide the sheep for the holocaust, in the person of his only Son, Jesus.

In the end, Abraham was not required to kill Isaac, but his willingness to do so led God to declare:

> Because you acted as you did in not withholding from me your beloved son, I will bless you abundantly and make your descendants as countless as the stars of the sky and the sands of the seashore; . . . and in your descendants all the nations of the earth shall find blessing—all this because you obeyed my command (Gen 22:16–18).

Isaac lived in the promised land, and so did his son Jacob and his grandsons, the "founders" of the twelve tribes that were to form the nation of Israel. But because of a famine, Isaac's descendants eventually moved to Egypt. At first they were treated well there; later, though, they were virtually enslaved for centuries.

God had not forgotten his promise to Abraham and his descendants, however. He raised up Moses for the rescue and liberation of his people and for their restoration to their land. It was a mighty act of deliverance that forever after stood as the great foreshadowing of the decisive and final deliverance to come.

The story is familiar but bears recounting. Its truths are endlessly rich, profound, and life-giving.

Pharaoh resisted Moses' demands that the Israelites be released and allowed to return to their own land. So God sent a succession of plagues as a judgment on Pharaoh's hardheartedness. Pharaoh stubbornly resisted them all. Then God decided to slay all the firstborn of the Egyptians throughout the entire land. He asked his people to gather in family groupings, to sacrifice a lamb and sprinkle its blood on their doorposts and lintels, to roast it, and then eat it together.

It is the Passover of the Lord. For on this same night I will go through Egypt, striking down every first-born of the land, both man and beast, and executing judgment on all the gods of Egypt—I, the Lord! But the blood will mark the houses where you are. Seeing the blood, I will pass over you; thus, when I strike the land of Egypt, no destructive blow will come upon you (Ex 12:11–13).

In this way the Lord rescued the Israelites. And he asked them to celebrate this passing over and deliverance as an annual feast, a reminder of what God had done for them.

But the Israelites' troubles were not over. Delivered from Egypt, they spent forty years wandering in the Sinai desert—grumbling, complaining, torn between the desire to be a free people and the longing for the miserable security they had known as slaves in Egypt. This hardheadedness delayed God's plan for them. Nevertheless, at Mount Sinai, God definitively established the Israelites as a nation. He gave them a way of life, revealed his Law, gave them the Ten Commandments. He showed forth his own glory and power and reaffirmed his covenant to them as a people.

It was Joshua who led the Israelites back into the promised land, Moses having fallen short of God's intentions for him. At first, judges ruled the people, and then kings, most of whom "did evil in the sight of the Lord" (1 Kings 11:6, for example) and shared in the general unfaithfulness of God's chosen people.

But because of his enduring love for mankind and for Israel, God sent prophets to call his people to return to him, to his mercy, truth, justice, and power. Although some responded to his call, the people largely ignored the prophets' message. Once again, Israel suffered the consequences of its disobedience — in exile, military defeats, occupation by the Romans, the final destruction of Jerusalem and its temple, and the dispersal of the people to the far corners of the earth.

As the prophets saw the Israelites turn from God and suffer defeat and humiliation, they began to prophesy of a future time when a more fundamental change would transform the inner nature of God's people. All would know God then, and he would establish a new and eternal covenant with them.

> The days are coming, says the Lord, when I will make a new covenant with the house of Israel and the house of Judah. . . . I will place my law within them, and write it upon their hearts; I will be their God, and they shall be my people. No longer will they have need to teach their friends and kinsmen how to know the Lord. All, from least to greatest, shall know me, says the Lord, for I will forgive their evildoing and remember their sin no more (Jer 31:31, 33–34).

Long before Isaiah spoke there had been a longing for just such a transformation. "Would that all the people of the Lord were prophets!" Moses had cried out. "Would that the Lord might bestow his spirit on them all!" (Num

11:29). Now, through the prophet Joel, God explicitly promised his people what Moses had so desired:

> Then afterward I will pour out
> my spirit upon all mankind.
> Your sons and daughters shall prophesy,
> your old men shall dream dreams,
> your young men shall see visions;
> Even upon the servants and the handmaids,
> in those days, I will pour out my spirit.

> (Joel 3:1)

Other prophets—Ezekiel and Jeremiah—tell of the day when God himself will come and be the good shepherd of his people, giving them personally and directly what the unfaithful shepherds of Israel withheld. This messianic king and shepherd—holy and righteous, descended from David—will restore and gather God's people.

> For thus says the Lord God: I myself will look after and tend my sheep. . . . I myself will pasture my sheep; I myself will give them rest. . . . I will appoint one shepherd over them to pasture them, my servant David; he shall pasture them and be their shepherd. I, the Lord, will be their God, and my servant David shall be prince among them. I, the Lord, have spoken (Ezek 34:11, 15, 23–24).

> Woe to the shepherds who mislead and scatter the flock of my pasture, says the Lord. . . . I myself will gather the remnant of my flock. . . .

Behold, the days are coming, says the Lord,
   when I will raise up a righteous shoot to David;
As king he shall reign and govern wisely,
   he shall do what is just and right in the land. . . .
This is the name they give him:
   "The Lord our justice"

                        (Jer 23:1, 3, 5, 6).

But there is another — and a grimmer — side to the prophetic word, indeed, to the whole story of God's dealings with the human race: the holy and righteous messengers and servants of God, sent by him or raised up by his grace, are an affront to fallen humanity and provoke its hatred. The Book of Wisdom provides a striking description of this hostility, one that is later seen by Matthew as directly predictive of Christ's Passion.

Let us beset the just one, because he is obnoxious
     to us;
   he sets himself against our doings,
Reproaches us for transgressions of the law
   and charges us with violations of our training.
He professes to have knowledge of God
   and styles himself a child of the Lord.
To us he is the censure of our thoughts;
   merely to see him is a hardship for us,
Because his life is not like other men's,
   and different are his ways.
He judges us debased;
   he holds aloof from our paths as from things
     impure.

He calls blest the destiny of the just
   and boasts that God is his Father.
Let us see whether his words be true;
   let us find out what will happen to him.
For if the just one be the son of God, he will
     defend him
   and deliver him from the hand of his foes.
With revilement and torture let us put him to
     the test
   that we may have proof of his gentleness
   and try his patience.
Let us condemn him to a shameful death;
   for according to his own words, God will take
   care of him.

(Wis 2:12–20; see also Mt 27:41–44)

Psalm 22 presents another gripping portrait of the just man confronted by hostility and then vindicated. Here again, the New Testament writers understood these verses as being fulfilled in a transcendent manner by Christ. But the Servant Songs of Isaiah (especially Isaiah 53, which we will examine later) give the most remarkable of these descriptions of the redemptive suffering of the just at the hands of fallen humanity.

One of Jesus' own parables best describes the situation of the human race on the eve of his coming. So far even the best had failed. Abraham had sinned, as had Noah; Moses, as well as David; the best had fallen short, and the human race was locked in its sin and misery. What remained for God to do?

He began to address them once more in parables: "A man planted a vineyard, put a hedge around it, dug out a vat, and erected a tower. Then he leased it to tenant farmers and went on a journey. In due time he dispatched a man in his service to the tenants to obtain from them his share of produce from the vineyard. But they seized him, beat him, and sent him off empty-handed. The second time he sent them another servant; him too they beat over the head and treated shamefully. He sent yet another and they killed him. So too with many others, some they beat; some they killed. He still had one to send — the son whom he loved. He sent him to them as a last resort, thinking, 'They will have to respect my son.' But those tenants said to one another, 'Here is the one who will inherit everything. Come, let us kill him, and the inheritance will be ours.' Then they seized and killed him and dragged him outside the vineyard. What do you suppose the owner of the vineyard will do? He will come and destroy those tenants and turn his vineyard over to others. Are you not familiar with this passage of Scripture:

> 'The stone rejected by the builders
>   has become the keystone of the structure.
> It was the Lord who did it
>   and we find it marvelous to behold'?"

(Mk 12:1–11)

FOUR

Another Beginning

In the beginning was the Word;
the Word was in God's presence,
and the Word was God. . . .
Through him all things came into being,
and apart from him nothing came to be. . . .
He was in the world,
and through him the world was made,
yet the world did not know who he was.
To his own he came,
yet his own did not accept him.
Any who did accept him
he empowered to become children of God.

— Jn 1:1, 3, 10–12

Scripture talks about the coming of God's Son in many ways, all of which shed light on the nature and purpose of his mission. The above passage from John underlines one aspect of his coming — that God came to us in Jesus so that we might pass from being fallen creatures to being actually sons and daughters of God.

A little later in his Gospel, John presents another way of viewing Jesus' coming: "Yes, God so loved the world that he gave his only Son, that whoever believes in him may not die but may have eternal life" (Jn 3:16). In other words, Jesus came to rescue us from the curse of death that had become our lot through the sin of the first man and woman; he established us in a new and remarkable form of life — eternal life.

Paul confirms and elaborates John's understanding concerning the coming of Christ: "But when the designated time had come, God sent forth his Son born of a woman, . . . so that we might receive our status as adopted sons. . . . You are no longer a slave but a son!" (Gal 4:4–5, 7).

Jesus, then, was the culmination of God's promise and plan to rescue the human race from the slavery it had entered. What was spoken through the prophets and prefigured in God's saving acts for the Jewish people — particularly their deliverance from Egypt — was fulfilled for all men in the coming of Christ. In Christ, God acted decisively, effectively, and finally for the liberation of the human race. As the Holy Spirit inspired the writer of Hebrews to put it:

In times past, God spoke in fragmentary and varied ways to our fathers through the prophets; in this, the final age, he has spoken to us through his Son, whom he has made heir of all things and through whom he first created the universe. This Son is the reflection of the Father's glory, the exact representation of the Father's being, and he sustains all things by his powerful word. When he had cleansed us from our sins, he took his seat at the right hand of the Majesty in heaven, as far superior to the angels as the name he has inherited is superior to theirs (Heb 1:1–4).

Jesus came into our midst and went about doing good: forgiving sin, overthrowing the power Satan and his demons had usurped, overcoming the effects of the rule of sin and Satan, healing the sick, raising the dead, giving sight to the blind and hearing to the deaf, teaching the truths concerning the kingdom of God.

It is remarkable enough — inconceivable, even — that God became man and dwelt among us. It is even more extraordinary that God-become-man, Jesus Christ, should allow himself to receive in his person all the accumulated hatred of a fallen race ruled by Satan, a hatred that was murderously hostile to the holiness of God.

Righteous men through the centuries had suffered and died because of this hostility. "Was there ever any prophet whom your fathers did not persecute?" asks Stephen just before his own martyrdom. "In their day, they put to death those who foretold the coming of the Just One" (Acts 7:52). In Jesus, this Just Man, announced by so many martyrs and prophets, took upon himself the sins of the world and endured the rage of the forces of hell. He was humiliated, tortured, subjected to a shameful death. And by his suffering and death, Jesus won for us the redemption spoken of by the prophets. His holy life literally fulfilled all the demands of the Law; his redemptive death and Resurrection fulfilled the hopes of the prophets in a manner beyond comprehension.

God's own Son underwent precisely and completely the sufferings prophesied in the Psalms, predicted of the Servant of Yahweh, and foretold in the fate of just men at the hands of the ungodly throughout the centuries. His life fulfilled what had been predicted of the messiah-king.

Jesus was born in Bethlehem (Micah 5:1) of a virgin (Is 7:14), an offshoot of David (Is 9:6). He was called out of Egypt (Hos 11:11) and preceded by a forerunner (Malachi 3:1). He ministered in Galilee (Is 9:1–2), was rejected by his own people (Is 53:3), entered Jerusalem riding on a donkey (Zech 9:9). Betrayed by a friend (Ps 41:10) and sold for thirty pieces of silver (Zech 11:12), Jesus was accused by false witnesses (Ps 35:11) but stood silent before these accusations (Is 53:7). He was spat upon and whipped (Is 50:6), considered a wrongdoer (Is 53:12), scorned and mocked (Ps 22:7–8), given vinegar and gall to drink (Ps 69:22). Men gambled for his garments (Ps 22:19), and he was pierced with a spear, yet none of his bones was broken (Zech 12:10; Ps 34:21).

However, unlike the just ones who preceded him, Jesus was raised from the dead (Ps 16:10; 49:16) and ascended on high (Ps 68:19).

Jesus embodied and fulfilled all the longing of Israel — everything spoken of by the prophets, represented in its great men and established in its institutions. But he did this in a way utterly without precedent, for this was God himself offering to suffer and die at our hands as a sacrifice for our sins.

Why did he do this? Why, we ask ourselves, gazing on the Cross and struck by the boundless depth of the question. Because the love of God for man was greater than any man could ever have conceived. Who would have dared to imagine the stunning mercy of the Incarnation and Passion? Would it not have bordered on blasphemy for man even to imagine such an idea, assuming that he could imagine it in the first place? Yet God himself breathed that Word; and when he did, it became not blasphemy but overwhelming mercy, grace, and love without measure.

Why the death of Christ? Why his Incarnation? Why did he empty himself, taking the form of a slave, submitting to the mockery and evil hostility of men, dying on the Cross? Jesus himself indicated one reason: "There is no greater love than this: to lay down one's life for one's friends" (Jn 15:13). God's love far surpasses even the greatest imaginings of man — for he loves even his enemies: "It is precisely in this that God proves his love for us: that while we were still sinners Christ died for us" (Rom 5:8). We may not understand it completely, but somehow, as the Letter to the Hebrews puts it, "it was fitting" that Jesus should undergo suffering and identify himself with fallen man (Heb 2:10).

What did the Incarnation, Passion, death, and Resurrection of the Son of God accomplish? Everything that was required to reconcile man to God — and more.

Consider the task before Jesus. Man had opted for evil, had freely chosen against God and broken his relationship with him. Now, when one party seriously injures another, their relationship cannot be restored unless the offender repents, acknowledges his sin, and takes measures to ensure that it will not be repeated. He must also make appropriate restitution for the injury already inflicted. Unless all of these elements are fulfilled, the relationship remains broken even if the injured party should wish to take the initiative and forgive; truth and justice must be satisfied.

God had never stopped loving man and was eager to welcome him back. Yet that reconciliation could never take place without adequate reparation on man's part. And what had man to offer? The Creator of the universe had been wronged. The rebellion had been fundamental, the damage grave, the consequences all-encompassing, the darkness of mind great, the corruption of will profound. The fall had given a foothold to the evil genius of Satan and his legions, and so evil had begotten more evil. The descendants of Abraham had been called to become as numerous as the sands of the sea or the stars of the sky, but so too had become their sins.

In the face of the overwhelming weight of sin throughout the ages, what could a human being — or even a group of human beings — ever do to express repentance and make restitution? How to expiate the intolerable burden of theft and murder, rape and falsehood, deception, war, violence, envy, jealousy, hostility, infidelity, adultery, blasphemy, idolatry, greed, oppression? How to make recompense for the fall itself, for its vast and incalculable damage, for the infernal evil it released into creation? What to present as appropriate satisfaction for the millennia of wars and pillage, genocide, infanticide, foul perversions, and corruption of children; for the oppression of the poor, the torture and slaughter of the innocent; for the Buchenwalds and Auschwitzes throughout the ages past and the ages to come; for the sin and horror of all time?

No man or group of men could hope to make recompense for these affronts to a holy God. Their restitution could never even have been imagined from within the human race, so enormous was our collective guilt, so personal our complicity, so deep-seated our inability to repent corporately or even personally.

What man could not do for himself, the Son, God-made-man, did for him. When we had nothing to give, Jesus took human form and offered himself freely as an acceptable sacrifice. Out of love, he descended to the depths, that we might ascend to the heights; he became man, that we might become as gods.

The Son of God led a life of perfect holiness, in utter obedience to the Father, for the sake of those who would be his brethren. He offered a blameless sacrifice as recompense for the millennia of horror and blasphemy, and he made intercession with a pure heart for the sins of the race. He gathered to himself in intensified form all the punishment accruing from the sin of all men in all ages, and he suffered in his own person the consequences of the fall and the rebellion of Satan.

The early councils of the Church defined and clarified the importance of Jesus' dual nature in this. He was truly man: the Son of Man, representative of our race, identified with us and therefore able to intercede as one of us. But he was also truly God: his was the holiest and purest of intercessions, the sacrifice of infinite value, the prayer of compelling strength.

Who could have fathomed the love of our God? Who

can ever fully grasp the significance of the death and Resurrection of God's Son?

> Who would believe what we have heard?
>> To whom has the arm of the Lord been revealed?
> He grew up like a sapling before him;
>> like a shoot from the parched earth;
> There was in him no stately bearing to make us look at him,
>> nor appearance that would attract us to him.
> He was spurned and avoided by men,
>> a man of suffering, accustomed to infirmity,
> One of those from whom men hide their faces,
>> spurned, and we held him in no esteem.
>
> Yet it was our infirmities that he bore,
>> our sufferings that he endured,
> While we thought of him as stricken,
>> as one smitten by God and afflicted.
> But he was pierced for our offenses,
>> crushed for our sins;
> Upon him was the chastisement that makes us whole,
>> by his stripes we were healed.
> We had all gone astray like sheep,
>> each following his own way;
> But the Lord laid upon him
>> the guilt of us all. . . .
>
> If he gives his life as an offering for sin,
>> he shall see his descendants in a long life,
>> and the will of the Lord shall be accomplished
>>> through him. . . .

Through his suffering, my servant shall justify many,
    and their guilt he shall bear. . . .
Because he surrendered himself to death
    and was counted among the wicked;
And he shall take away the sins of many,
    and win pardon for their offenses.

(Is 53:1–6, 10, 11, 12)

Jesus Christ won for us our salvation. It was he who gave his life "as an offering for sin". He endured the suffering that came from our sin, the guilt that resulted from our rebellion, the infirmities and weaknesses that stemmed from our wrongdoing. Because he was "pierced for our offenses" and "crushed for our sins", he is able now to "justify many", to "take away the sins of many, and win pardon for their offenses".

The intercession of the Just One, the suffering and death of the Holy One, the blood of the Son of God, can wash away and make new; it can justify, cleanse, and restore; it erases the atrocities and the crimes of a race's history. As enormous as the guilt and crimes of all humanity are, more enormous yet is the value of the blood of God's own Son as it pleads for forgiveness, for a new beginning, for another chance. The enormity of the offering made for sin, the blood of God, overshadows the numbing enormity of the sin of the ages.

Because Christ's life, suffering, and death were pleasing in the eyes of God, because he was a worthy recompense and restitution for our sins, the human race was offered a new start. As all fell in Adam, so in Christ were all offered the chance to renounce the fall and begin again.

Through his death and Resurrection, Christ became the foundation stone on which the human race was refounded. Jesus became the beachhead of the reign of God in a fallen world, the first dwelling place of salvation, the firstborn of the dead, the firstborn of many brothers. Men and women who clung to him and became part of him — members of his body and partakers of his Body and Blood — shared in the effects of his life, death, and Resurrection. If we trust Jesus, believe in him, place our hopes in him, and follow and obey him, God stands ready to forgive our sins and free us from our bondage to Satan. This surrender is expressed and effected in the sacramental participation in the death and Resurrection of Christ in the sacraments of baptism and Eucharist. From then on, we can count ourselves as his adopted sons and daughters, new men and women filled with God's own Spirit. We have become dead to sin and alive to God, partakers in the divine nature, heirs to Christ's own inheritance, and destined, like him, for resurrection and eternal life.

Critical as the Passion and death of Christ are, they represent only one dimension of the salvation God has wrought for us. There is another: the Resurrection. God did not let his Holy One see corruption but raised him up to his right hand. As we have seen, some of the psalms tell of this. And even in the midst of Isaiah's Servant Songs, the manifest victory of the Servant of God is proclaimed:

> See, my servant shall prosper,
>   he shall be raised high and greatly exalted.
> Even as many were amazed at him —

so marred was his look beyond that of man,
    and his appearance beyond that of mortals—
So shall he startle many nations,
    because of him kings shall stand speechless;
For those who have not been told shall see,
    those who have not heard shall ponder it.

(Is 52:13–15)

And again, consider Psalm 22, the psalm of Christ's Passion whose opening lines Jesus recited on the Cross: "My God, my God, why have you forsaken me?" Besides foreshadowing many of the specific aspects of Christ's agony, the psalm concludes in a glorious affirmation of the Messiah's victory through suffering:

All the ends of the earth
    shall remember and turn to the Lord;
All the families of the nations
    shall bow down before him.
For dominion is the Lord's,
    and he rules the nations. . . .
Let the coming generation be told of the Lord
    that they may proclaim to a people yet to be born
    the justice he has shown.

(Ps 22:28–29, 31–32)

Chapter 2 of the Book of Wisdom presents the suffering and death of the Just One at the hands of the ungodly, but chapter 5 of the same book recounts his triumph:

Then shall the just one with great assurance confront
   his oppressors who set at naught his labors.
Seeing this, they shall be shaken with dreadful fear,
   and amazed at the unlooked-for salvation.
They shall say among themselves, rueful
   and groaning through anguish of spirit:
"This is he whom once we held as a laughingstock
   and as a type for mockery, fools that we were!
His life we accounted madness,
   and his death dishonored.
See how he is accounted among the sons of God;
   how his lot is with the saints!

(Wis 5:1–5)

The Old Testament anticipates the Resurrection of Jesus;
the triumphant cry resounds throughout its pages. "The
joyful shout of victory [arises] in the tents of the just",
Psalm 118 declares, because in the Resurrection, "the right
hand of the Lord has struck with power: the right hand of
the Lord is exalted; the right hand of the Lord has struck
with power" (vv. 15–16). And because of the Resurrection, those who join themselves to Christ can profess: "I
shall not die, but live, and declare the works of the Lord.
Though the Lord has indeed chastised me, yet he has not
delivered me to death" (vv. 17–18).

The stone which the builders rejected
   has become the cornerstone.
By the Lord has this been done;
   it is wonderful in our eyes.

This is the day the Lord has made;
let us be glad and rejoice in it.

(Ps 118:22–24)

Because of the Resurrection, the hopes of the holy ones
of old find fulfillment; the startling faith of Job is fulfilled:
"I know that my redeemer liveth . . . and I shall behold
him in the flesh, even though I die, standing before me"
(Job 19:25, 26).

The Resurrection manifests the Father's acceptance of
his Son's sacrifice on behalf of the human race. It shows
us that Satan has been overthrown, the curse of sin and
death lifted, the Spirit of God bestowed. The Resurrection
assures us that all flesh can be saved and creation itself redeemed. Because of it we can know that we "shall not die,
but live, and declare the works of the Lord" (Ps 118:17).
Finally, the Resurrection provides a glimpse of what awaits
those who are joined to Christ and enables us to celebrate
the only victory that really matters: the defeat of our final
enemy, death.

Christ is now raised from the dead, the first fruits of
those who have fallen asleep. Death came through
a man; hence the resurrection of the dead comes
through a man also. Just as in Adam all die, so in
Christ all will come to life again, but each one in
proper order: Christ the first fruits and then, at his
coming, all those who belong to him. . . . When the
corruptible frame takes on incorruptibility and the
mortal immortality, then will the saying of Scripture be fulfilled: "Death is swallowed up in victory."

"O death, where is your victory? O death, where is your sting?" The sting of death is sin, and sin gets its power from the law. But thanks be to God who has given us the victory through our Lord Jesus Christ (1 Cor 15:20–23, 54–57).

The life, Passion, death, and Resurrection of Jesus more than satisfied the requirements of our reconciliation with God. Although all men must still pass through physical death (a consequence of sin and the fall that has not been lifted yet), the *sting* of death for a Christian has been removed. The sting of death is sin, which leads to eternal separation from God. For a Christian, however, the forgiveness of sins has removed this sting, and death becomes a passageway to everlasting joy in the presence of God. For the sake of men Jesus laid down his life before the Father, an offering of infinite value. The Father, in turn, has put everything into Jesus' charge. He has given him all authority to work through his disciples in proclaiming this saving good news and to gather to the Father all those who accept his work, appropriate it personally, and join themselves to him. God promises to bestow on them—now, as a foretaste, but in its fullness at his coming in glory—the same Spirit who worked in and through Jesus and raised him from the dead.

The salvation of the human race is not a game or an intellectual or linguistic exercise. It is real, historical, factual. Man really sinned and experienced extremely tangible consequences. Something real and extraordinary had to happen to repair the vastness and enormity of the sin.

This real and extraordinary atonement was accomplished in history in the death and Resurrection of Jesus. This opened up a new beginning, another chance to escape the futility of a life lived in sin, ruled by Satan, destined for death and eternal misery. God offers us this new chance under the same conditions as the first—that is, we are free to choose. The first man and woman, and all of us in them, freely chose to turn from God and to revolt against the order of the universe. Now Christ has made it possible to choose anew, and this means that each of us can reject the sin of our first parents, freely choose to turn back to God, repent of our sin and rebellion, and ask for forgiveness and pardon.

But the wrong choice remains possible too. Just as the first man and woman rejected God's first plan, so too can we reject the new beginning. In the event of another wrong choice, however, there remains no hope.

Christ's death and Resurrection—the new chance for the human race—is also the last chance. Nothing more can be done or given than what has been done and given in Christ. The Son of God offers us all that is required and more. Nothing more can be done if individuals and groups reject his salvation and refuse to submit to the reign of God brought close to us in the person of Jesus. Such people condemn themselves; they will die in their sins and will be raised at the glorious coming of Christ only for judgment and "the second death" (Rev 20:6).

The coming of Christ is good news for all those who are prepared to repent, ask pardon, submit to the reign of God, and be joined to his body. But for those who persist in rebellion, his coming is the occasion for their judgment.

Pardon and mercy are offered to those who hear the call of the crucified and resurrected Christ—that extraordinary "last cry of love" to a perishing race, as John Paul II has put it—and come to him for forgiveness and new life. Judgment and condemnation are reserved for those who gaze upon the Cross, hear testimony of the Resurrection, and receive the light and witness of the Holy Spirit, only to persist in their sins.

Jesus Christ is the only way of salvation offered to the human race; none bypasses him or exists apart from him. To be in Christ and with Christ is to be saved; not to be in him is to be lost. Apart from Christ, the greatest enlightenment is only darkness. All who do not walk in his light do not see, for the very person of Christ, crucified and risen, is the source of light. Light is given to see Christ. If men do not see Christ, there is only darkness.

We see overwhelming love in the death and Resurrection of Jesus, and we also see extraordinary justice. As Catherine of Siena said, the death of God's own Son is no joke. Something awful happened to require it, and something awful happens if we reject it. Now that Christ has come, the prospects for the human race are both much brighter and much more perilous.

> For if the word spoken through angels stood unchanged, and all transgression and disobedience received its due punishment, how shall we escape if we ignore a salvation as great as ours? Announced first by the Lord, it was confirmed to us by those who had heard him. God then gave witness to it by signs,

miracles, varied acts of power, and distribution of the gifts of the Holy Spirit as he willed (Heb 2:2–4).

As Christ ascends to the Father, he leaves us with a sobering commission that underlines the serious consequences: "Go into the whole world and proclaim the good news to all creation. The man who believes in it and accepts baptism will be saved; the man who refuses to believe in it will be condemned" (Mk 16:15–16).

The Christian gospel is a gospel with consequences. Our response to God's offer in the death and Resurrection of Jesus makes an eternal difference. Jesus came the first time as a lamb to take away the sins of the world by his sacrificial death. But he is coming again, this time as king and judge of the entire race. Being prepared for his Second Coming is as important as being prepared for his first. Just as his First Coming was prophetically predicted in extraordinary detail, so too is his Second Coming described in considerable detail. Just as the prophecies of his First Coming were fulfilled, so will be the prophecies of his Second Coming—with implications for all our lives.

Today, when presentations of the gospel are often vague, it is very important to know how specific and concrete the word of God is. Let us now turn to a consideration of what the gospel says about Jesus' Second Coming.

FIVE

The Return of the Lord

He will come again in glory to judge the living and the dead, and his kingdom will have no end.

— Nicene Creed

These words from the ancient Creed reflect in a condensed form the teaching of Scripture regarding the return of the Lord.[1]

Christ came once into our midst as a servant, a slave, a lamb sacrificed for us. He will come again — but the second time he will come in glory to establish definitively his reign over the human race. The first time, he came as God's offer of full salvation; the second time, he will come to judge how the human race has responded to that offer. To those who have put their trust in him, he will give the fullness of salvation; those who have persisted

[1] Volume 6 of Michael Schmaus' work *Dogma: Justification and the Last Things* (Kansas City and London: Sheed and Ward, 1977), 177–274, contains a useful overview of the Scripture, history of the development of doctrine, official Catholic Church teaching, and contemporary theological debate about the topics discussed in this book pertaining to the Second Coming and the associated topics.

in wrongdoing, who have rejected him, his word, and his servants, will be banished from his presence.

> Just as it is appointed that men die once, and after death be judged, so Christ was offered up once to take away the sins of many; he will appear a second time not to take away sin but to bring salvation to those who eagerly await him (Heb 9:27–28).

Jesus himself frequently referred to his return in glory. "Then men will see the Son of Man coming in the clouds with great power and glory", he told his disciples. "He will dispatch his angels and assemble his chosen from the four winds, from the farthest bounds of earth and sky" (Mk 13:26–27). At Jesus' Ascension, it was angels who assured the disciples of Jesus' return: " 'Men of Galilee,' they said, 'why do you stand here looking up at the skies? This Jesus who has been taken from you will return, just as you saw him go up into the heavens' " (Acts 1:11).

This firm, clear belief in Jesus' visible and glorious return in power, as king and judge, is consistently taught and proclaimed throughout the New Testament. Along with the resurrection of the dead, it forms an integral part of the apostolic teaching and preaching:[2]

> I charge you to keep God's command without blame or reproach until our Lord Jesus Christ shall appear. This appearance God will bring to pass at his chosen time (1 Tim 6:14–15).

> Be patient, therefore, my brothers, until the coming of the Lord. . . . Steady your hearts, because the com-

---

[2] *Catechism of the Catholic Church* (hereafter CCC), 668–77.

ing of the Lord is at hand. Do not grumble against one another, my brothers, lest you be condemned. See! The judge stands at the gate (James 5:7, 8–9).

Just as in Adam all die, so in Christ all will come to life again, but each one in proper order: Christ the first fruits and then, at his coming, all those who belong to him (1 Cor 15:22–23).

From the standpoint of Scripture, living in expectancy of Christ's coming — indeed, longing for it! — is an essential element of Christian life itself. "From now on a merited crown awaits me", Paul tells Timothy. "On that Day the Lord, just judge that he is, will award it to me — and not only to me, but to all who have looked for his appearing with eager longing" (2 Tim 4:8). Paul also urges all Christians to encourage one another with the truth that Jesus will come again:

No, the Lord himself will come down from heaven at the word of command, at the sound of the archangel's voice and God's trumpet. . . . Thenceforth we shall be with the Lord unceasingly. Console one another with this message (1 Th 4:16, 17).

What Will His Coming Be Like?

It will be sudden and unexpected. Paul tells the Thessalonians:

You know very well that the day of the Lord is coming like a thief in the night. Just when people are

saying, "Peace and security," ruin will fall on them
with the suddenness of pains overtaking a woman in
labor, and there will be no escape (1 Th 5:2–3).

The human race as a whole will not be ready for Jesus'
return and will be caught by surprise. The Second Coming will not be — as some suggest — a logical progression of
the spiritual evolution of human consciousness, growing
into a fuller awareness of Jesus' presence with us. Scripture
presents quite a different picture:

> The coming of the Son of Man will repeat what hap-
> pened in Noah's time. In the days before the flood
> people were eating and drinking, marrying and being
> married, right up to the day Noah entered the ark.
> They were totally unconcerned until the flood came
> and destroyed them. So will it be at the coming of
> the Son of Man (Mk 24:37–39).

Christ's coming will be personal, clearly manifest, un-
mistakable, and visible to all. It will not be hidden or invisibly "spiritual"; this will be the incarnate Son coming,
not an invisible working of the Holy Spirit:

> Remember, I have told you all about it beforehand;
> so if they tell you, "Look, he is in the desert," do not
> go out there; or "He is in the innermost rooms," do
> not believe it. As the lightning from the east flashes
> to the west, so will the coming of the Son of Man
> be. . . . The sign of the Son of Man will appear in
> the sky, and "all the clans of the earth will strike
> their breasts" as they see "the Son of Man coming

on the clouds of heaven" with power and great glory (Mt 24:25–27, 30).

As the angels said at the Ascension, Jesus will return in the same personal, clearly visible, and manifest way in which he ascended to the Father. One will not need to go to special places or to engage in certain activities in order to see him and recognize his coming: it will be clear and unmistakably manifest to all.

When Will His Second Coming Take Place?

No One Knows the Day or Hour. Scripture clearly and specifically affirms that no one knows the day or hour of the Lord's return: "As to the exact day or hour, no one knows it, neither the angels in heaven nor even the Son, but only the Father" (Mk 13:32). In one of the post-Resurrection appearances, Jesus' disciples again asked him: " 'Lord, are you going to restore the rule to Israel now?' He answered: 'The exact time is not yours to know. The Father has reserved that to himself' " (Acts 1:6–7).

Paul reaffirms this in his apostolic teaching: "As regards specific times and moments, brothers, we do not need to write you; you know very well that the day of the Lord is coming like a thief in the night" (1 Th 5:1–2).

Nevertheless, Be Alert. While Scripture insists that we do not know the exact time of the Second Coming, it also insists that Christians should nonetheless lead lives of holiness and Christian service so that they will be prepared to be joined to Jesus when he does return. While the world as a whole will be "asleep" when the Lord returns, Christians are supposed to be "awake" and alert to his coming.

Usually the same passages say both things — do not worry about the exact time but also be alert. For example, in the post-Resurrection passage cited above, Jesus follows his correction — "The exact time is not yours to know" — with commissioning the disciples to witness to him: "You will receive power when the Holy Spirit comes down on you; then you are to be my witnesses in Jerusalem, throughout Judea and Samaria, yes, even to the ends of the earth" (Acts 1:8).

In another passage Jesus adds an exhortation to his teaching on the unknowability of the exact hour of his coming: "Be constantly on the watch! Stay awake! . . . Do not let him [the master of the house] come suddenly and catch you asleep. What I say to you, I say to all: Be on guard!" (Mk 13:33, 36–37).

Paul gives a similar warning to the Thessalonians and defines what it means to stay awake.

> You are not in the dark, brothers, that the day should catch you off guard, like a thief. No, all of you are children of light and of the day. We belong neither to darkness nor to night; therefore let us not be asleep like the rest, but awake and sober! . . . We who live by day must be alert, putting on faith and love as a breastplate and the hope of salvation as a helmet. . . . [C]omfort and upbuild one another. . . .
>
> Respect those among you whose task it is to exercise authority in the Lord and admonish you. . . .
>
> Rejoice always, never cease praying, render con-

stant thanks; such is God's will for you in Christ Jesus.

Do not stifle the Spirit. Do not despise prophecies. Test everything; retain what is good. Avoid any semblance of evil (1 Th 5:4–6, 8, 11, 12, 16–22).

How should we stay awake and not be caught off guard when Jesus returns? Paul's answer can be summed up this way: live a fervent Christian life, with everything that this entails.

Don't Be Thrown off Guard by Apparent Delays in His Coming. Scripture warns us not to trust our shortsighted human judgments about relative lengths of times. This might cause us to lose hope or become cynical or indifferent regarding the reality of Jesus' return:

Note this first of all: in the last days, mocking, sneering men who are ruled by their passions will arrive on the scene. They will ask: "Where is that promised coming of his? Our forefathers have been laid to rest, but everything stays just as it was when the world was created." In believing this, they do not take into account that of old there were heavens and an earth drawn out of the waters and standing between the waters, all brought into being by the word of God. By water that world was then destroyed; it was overwhelmed by the deluge. The present heavens and earth are reserved by God's word for fire; they are kept for the day of judgment, the day when godless men will be destroyed.

This point must not be overlooked, dear friends.

In the Lord's eyes, one day is as a thousand years and a thousand years are as a day. The Lord does not delay in keeping his promise — though some consider it "delay." Rather, he shows you generous patience, since he wants none to perish but all to come to repentance. The day of the Lord will come like a thief, and on that day the heavens will vanish with a roar; the elements will be destroyed by fire, and the earth and all its deeds will be made manifest.

Since everything is to be destroyed in this way, what sort of men must you not be! How holy in your conduct and devotion, looking for the coming of the day of God and trying to hasten it! Because of it, the heavens will be destroyed in flames and the elements will melt away in a blaze. What we await are new heavens and a new earth where, according to his promise, the justice of God will reside (2 Pet 3:3–13).

Here Peter warns Christians not to be taken in by a cynical attitude toward the apparent "delay" of the Lord's return. He points out that God has already cleansed the world of sin once, by the flood, and that he will purify it again on the Day of his coming, by fire. In the light of eternity, Peter maintains, it is simply not meaningful to talk about lengths of time and delays. Notice too that the apostle follows this teaching with the usual exhortation to prepare for the Lord's coming by leading lives of holiness; he even implies that the great Day can be hastened by an increase in the holiness of God's people.

While Scripture clearly says that the exact time or hour of the Lord's coming cannot be known and will not be revealed to man, it does shed some light on the matter, as a help for Christians being "awake" and alert to his coming. First of all, it indicates that certain events need to take place before Jesus' return. Second, it points out some conditions that will prevail in the world and among God's people just before his coming and that will serve as proximate warnings for those who are alert to them.

Preliminary Events

Scripture singles out two events that are going to take place before history is concluded in the Lord's coming. One is the completion of the time of the Gentiles and the conversion of Israel; the other is the proclamation of the gospel to all nations.

The Conversion of Israel. Paul indicates that God's plan includes a time when Israel as a whole will be saved.[3]

> For if their rejection has meant reconciliation for the world, what will their [the Jews'] acceptance mean? Nothing less than life from the dead! . . . And if the Jews do not remain in their unbelief they will be grafted back on, for God is able to do this. . . . Brothers, I do not want you to be ignorant of this mystery lest you be conceited; blindness has come upon part of Israel until the full number of Gentiles enter

[3] CCC, 674.

in, and then all Israel will be saved (Rom 11:15, 23, 25–26).

In this chapter of Romans, Paul indicates that the Jews' disobedience and rejection of the gospel has opened up the way for the gospel to spread among non-Jews. For a time, he says, it is mainly the Gentiles who will receive the good news, but this phase of evangelistic activity will eventually reach its completion. Then will begin the next phase of God's plan of salvation—the conversion of Israel.

Another passage that is relevant here is Luke 21:24. This passage clearly indicates that Jerusalem will be "trampled down" under Gentile control after its destruction until the times of the Gentiles are fulfilled:

> The people will fall before the sword; they will be led captive in the midst of the Gentiles. Jerusalem will be trampled by the Gentiles, until the times of the Gentiles are fulfilled.

Jerusalem was destroyed in A.D. 70. The city was under substantially non-Jewish control from that time until 1967, when it was retaken by the Jewish state in the Six-Day War. Jerusalem is not under Israel's absolute control, but it is under Jewish governmental authority for the first time since the Romans destroyed it. It may be that the "times of the Gentiles"—the period during which Jerusalem is under Gentile control—are in the process of coming to an end.

In light of this, it is certainly significant that the Jewish people are now back in the Holy Land and since 1947 reconstituted as a nation for the first time since the destruction of Jerusalem and the temple and their own dispersal (predicted by Jesus as a sign of God's judgment on them for rejecting him). It is also significant that since 1967 Jerusalem has been under their control. At the same time, let us bear in mind that Israel is a very secular state, with vast numbers of its citizens not even practicing seriously the Jewish faith. While its existence once again as a state and the retaking of Jerusalem are probably not without spiritual significance, it does not follow necessarily that God is pleased with its treatment of the Palestinians, for example. That's a question that needs to be approached on other grounds. It is important that we pray that Israel will play the role God wants it to play in his plan.

It appears that the full number of Gentile Christians has not been reached, although the time of the Gentiles may be coming to an end, and that God has also begun to set the scene for a significant dealing with Israel.

The Universal Proclamation of the Gospel. Jesus himself said that the gospel would be proclaimed to all the nations before he would come again. "Only after that will the end come" (Mt 24:14).

It is difficult to know whether this universal proclamation has taken place. Certain nations have had the gospel preached to them in the past but not in the present. This was the case in the former communist countries. North Africa, too, had a very substantial Christian population at one time, but now it is primarily Moslem, with Christian witness virtually nonexistent in most of these countries. China was once a thriving mission field for Christians, with some of its emperors in special contact with the Jesuits, but relatively few modern Chinese have heard the gospel of Christ. And there are countries where the Christian population has always been relatively small—India, for example. Has the Christian presence there been long and visible enough to constitute a proclamation of the gospel to the nation?

On the other hand, the last century has seen a remarkable intensification of missionary activity on the part of the Christian churches. For example, a hundred years or so ago the Christian population of Africa was estimated at about half a million. Today, authoritative estimates place it at about three hundred million.

Despite this remarkable advance, the World Mission Center and others who have closely studied the situation estimate that perhaps two billion people still have not been adequately evangelized. This includes thousands of distinct tribal, ethnic, and national groups, primarily in Moslem, Buddhist, and Hindu countries.

It seems safe to say that there has indeed been an extraordinary preaching of the gospel throughout the world since Jesus first preached in Galilee. But it also seems that at least today this evangelization has not yet reached the universality required to claim that all men have heard the gospel. At the same time, it is worth noting that virtually the whole world is wired into a global communication network that allows almost instant television and radio communication. In fact, a spiritual struggle is taking place over the use of such media for or against the kingdom of God. It is possible that many of the two billion who have never heard the gospel could hear it by means of this global communications network.

Even in my own limited experience I have seen what almost have to be called "miraculous" developments in the capacity to preach the gospel to all the world. For the past fourteen years my collaborators and I have produced and hosted a weekly television and radio program called "The Choices We Face". It has been one of the most widely distributed Catholic television programs. For most of that time we have worked closely with Mother Angelica's Eternal Word Television Network.

Seeing, firsthand, the development of this network "from nothing" has been an amazing experience. A cloistered nun in the deep South, through prayer, faith, and aggressive action, has helped bring into being what is quickly becoming a truly global Catholic television network. It is now transmitting to most of South America and Europe in addition to North America and, as I write this, is inaugurating an Asian capacity. The Scripture passage that influenced the naming of the network and its mission is from the Book of Revelation.

> Then I saw another angel flying in midheaven, with an eternal gospel to proclaim to those who dwell on earth, to every nation and tribe and tongue and people (Rev 14:6).

Proximate Signs

In addition to singling out the above events as preliminary to the return of the Lord, Scripture describes a se-

ries of difficulties and disorders that will function as proximate signs of the final days. These difficulties and disorders are sometimes referred to collectively as "the great
tribulation" (see Dan 12:1; Mk 13:19; Rev 16:18).

The descriptions of these signs in the synoptic Gospels
are hard to sort out because they are intermingled with
predictions about the impending destruction of Jerusalem.
Recent Scripture scholarship helps us understand which
elements in these passages refer to the destruction of
Jerusalem and which to the final coming of the Lord. At
the same time, Scripture scholars increasingly recognize
that the interplay between these perspectives and events is
significant and not just the result of an editorial jumbling.
For example, the catastrophic destruction of Jerusalem in
A.D. 70, which Jesus had predicted as God's judgment on
the Jews, is a foreshadowing of the final judgment to be
inaugurated by Jesus at his Second Coming.

We will now consider what the Gospels and the other
New Testament writings present as some of the distinct
elements of the disorder that will precede the coming of
Christ. These elements can be grouped under three head-
ings: general disorder among the nations and in nature;
confusion and division within the Church; and the rise
and work of the antichrist.

General Disorder. General disorder among the nations of
the world, coupled with widespread "natural disasters",
will inaugurate the beginning of the tribulation that will
precede the Lord's coming:

> You will hear of wars and rumors of wars. Do not be
> alarmed. Such things are bound to happen, but that

is not yet the end. Nation will rise against nation, one kingdom against another. There will be famine and pestilence and earthquakes in many places. These are the early stages of the birth pangs (Mt 24:6-8).

Note that these disorders are referred to as the "early stages of the birth pangs". This is an important perspective for Christians to have. In the midst of the turmoil and suffering, Christians are given a key to understanding that leads to hope and joy rather than fear and despair. An age in rebellion against God, a world distorted and perverted by sin, is perishing. But something new is coming to birth — a "new heavens and new earth", where the holiness of God will dwell, where there will be no more sorrow, no more sin, no more death.

In fact, Jesus told his disciples regarding the impending tribulation, "When these things begin to happen, stand erect and hold your heads high, for your deliverance is near at hand" (Lk 21:28).

The end of this period of severe tribulation will be marked by an intensification of the disorders and then the return of the Lord:

Immediately after the stress of that period, "the sun will be darkened, the moon will not shed her light, the stars will fall from the sky, and the hosts of heaven will be shaken loose." Then the sign of the Son of Man will appear in the sky, and "all the clans of the earth will strike their breasts" as they see "the Son of Man coming on the clouds of heaven" with power and great glory (Mt 24:29-30).

Confusion and Disorder in the Church. Another element of disorder that will precede Christ's coming is disorder in the Church. First, there will be disloyalty. The nations of the world will turn against the Christian people in a concerted way, creating a pressure that will reveal the quality of commitment and relationships that exist among Christians. Some Christians will yield to the provocations and will openly turn against one another and betray one another to the secular, anti-Christian authorities:

> They will hand you over to torture and kill you. Indeed, you will be hated by all nations on my account. Many will falter then, betraying and hating one another (Mt 24:9–10).

> Brother will hand over brother for execution and likewise the father his child; children will turn against their parents and have them put to death (Mk 13:12).

> Because of the increase of evil, the love of most will grow cold (Mt 24:12).

The horrifying slaughter in Rwanda, the most Catholic nation in Africa, where Catholics slaughtered Catholics in a frenzy of tribal fear and revenge, provides a startling picture of what the collapse of Christian life can look like today.

Another feature of the great tribulation will be the appearance of false teachers, prophets, and messiahs. They will preach a gospel different from the one of orthodox Christianity and will mislead many not firmly rooted in the faith:

While he was seated on the Mount of Olives, his disciples came up to him privately and said: "Tell us, when will all this occur? What will be the sign of your coming and the end of the world?" In reply Jesus said to them: "Be on guard! Let no one mislead you. Many will come attempting to impersonate me. 'I am the Messiah!' they will claim, and they will deceive many. . . . False prophets will rise in great numbers to mislead many. . . . False messiahs and false prophets will appear, performing signs and wonders so great as to mislead even the chosen if that were possible. Remember, I have told you all about it beforehand; so, if they tell you, 'Look, he is in the desert,' do not go out there; or 'He is in the innermost rooms,' do not believe it" (Mt 24:3–5, 24–26).

Do not forget this: there will be terrible times in the last days. Men will be lovers of self and of money, proud, arrogant, abusive, disobedient to their parents, ungrateful, profane, inhuman, implacable, slanderous, licentious, brutal, hating the good. They will be treacherous, reckless, pompous, lovers of pleasure rather than of God as they make a pretense of religion but negate its power. . . . Just as Jannes and Jambres opposed Moses, so these men also oppose the truth; with perverted minds they falsify the faith (2 Tim 3:1–5, 8).

The Spirit distinctly says that in later times some will turn away from the faith and will heed deceitful spir-

its and things taught by demons through plausible
liars (1 Tim 4:1).

Persecution, disorder in the Church, and confusion
about fundamental Christian truths perpetrated by false
teachers, prophets, and messiahs will take their toll: there
will be widespread desertion of the true Christian faith.
As Paul exhorts the Thessalonians:

> On the question of the coming of our Lord Jesus
> Christ and our being gathered to him, we beg you,
> brothers, not to be so easily agitated or terrified,
> whether by an oracular utterance, or rumor, or a let-
> ter alleged to be ours, into believing that the day of
> the Lord is here.
>
> Let no one seduce you, no matter how. Since
> the mass apostasy has not yet occurred . . . (2 Th
> 2:1-3).

At one point Jesus expressed great concern about what
condition his people would be in at his return: "But when
the Son of Man comes," Jesus asked his disciples, "will he
find any faith on the earth?" (Lk 18:8).

Has the mass apostasy occurred? Is it occurring now?
Certainly many statistical measurements of the state of
the Catholic Church, the Orthodox Church, and many
of the Reformation Protestant churches would lead one to
wonder. Many of the traditionally Catholic and Christian
nations in Europe, the Americas, and Oceania have seen
the collapse of Christian influence on culture, the law, the
universities, popular entertainment, marriage, and family
life. Only a relatively small percentage of nominal Cath-

olics in many countries even go to church anymore, and the same is true of many traditionally Protestant countries as well.

For example, in the United States church attendance among Catholics in the 1960s was about 75 percent; today it is about 28 percent. In Western Europe and Latin America the figures of current church attendance are generally much worse. Even in an extraordinarily strong Catholic country like Poland, which lived to see the collapse of communism, church attendance has dropped dramatically. Church attendance under communism just before it collapsed in 1989 was about 75 percent. Just four years later, in 1993, attendance was only about 28 percent nationally, and in the city of Warsaw only 18 percent. The collapse that took thirty years in the United States took only four years in Poland. The power of Western secularism is accomplishing what communism could not. Yet it is not just a matter of a devastating decline in church attendance. It is also a matter of the "spirit of the age" replacing the "mind of Christ" in many Church members. For example, in 1963, only 13 percent of U.S. Catholics thought that premarital sex was permissible. In 1974, 52 percent thought it was permissible, and in 1987, 71 percent.

The international pagan culture that is now aggressively spreading throughout the world is devastating the traditional Christian churches. Seventeen hundred years of Christendom is collapsing around us and is being replaced by an aggressive and militant relativism.[4]

---

[4] An extensive survey of these statistics on a worldwide basis is con-

The Rise of the Antichrist. In his first two epistles, John refers to the apparently common belief among Christians of his day that the antichrist would appear before the Lord's coming. He indicates that the false teachers operating at the time of his writing could be viewed as many such antichrists:

> Children, it is the final hour;
> just as you heard that the antichrist was coming,
> so now many such antichrists have appeared.
> This makes us certain that it is the final hour.
> It was from our ranks that they took their leave —
> not that they really belonged to us;
> for if they had belonged to us,
> they would have stayed with us.
> It only served to show that none of them was ours. . . .
> Who is the liar?
> He who denies that Jesus is the Christ.
> He is the antichrist,
> denying the Father and the Son.
> Anyone who denies the Son
> has no claim on the Father,
> but he who acknowledges the Son
> can claim the Father as well.
>
> (1 Jn 2:18–19, 22–23)

Here, for John, the "final hour" is the final age of the world — the time between the First and Second Com-

---

tained in chapter 2 of my book *The Catholic Church at the End of an Age: What Is the Spirit Saying?*, San Francisco: Ignatius Press, 1994.

ings of Christ. The antichrists, false teachers, and false prophets have emerged from within the ranks of the Christian churches and are distorting the heart of the gospel message. One thrust of the antichrist's teaching is to deny that Jesus truly is the Son of God, Savior and Lord, the Christ. Another element of this false teaching is to deny that it is necessary to go through Jesus to reach a relationship with God the Father. In short, the false teachers reject the universal necessity and relevance of the role of Jesus in God's plan:

> Beloved,
> do not trust every spirit,
> but put the spirits to a test
> to see if they belong to God,
> because many false prophets have appeared in
>   the world.
> This is how you can recognize God's Spirit:
> every spirit that acknowledges Jesus Christ come
>   in the flesh
> belongs to God,
> while every spirit that fails to acknowledge him
> does not belong to God.
> Such is the spirit of the antichrist
> which, as you have heard, is to come;
> in fact, it is in the world already.
> You are of God, you little ones,
> and thus you have conquered the false prophets.
> For there is One greater in you
> than there is in the world.
> Those others belong to the world;

that is why theirs is the language of the world
and why the world listens to them.

(1 Jn 4:1–5)

These verses of John are reminiscent of what Paul tells
the Corinthians: "That is why I tell you that nobody who
speaks in the Spirit of God ever says, 'Cursed be Jesus.'
And no one can say: 'Jesus is Lord,' except in the Holy
Spirit" (1 Cor 12:3). The formulas offered here by Paul
and John are not foolproof methods of discerning true
from false, to be used in a legalistic way. For example,
someone could very well profess verbally "Jesus is Lord"
or "Jesus came in the flesh", while twisting the meaning
of those phrases to mean the very opposite. The point of
these warnings is to guard against the antichrist's strategy
of undermining foundational Christian truths such as the
Incarnation and the unique role and identity of Jesus as
Savior of the entire race and the only way to the Father.

The early Church considered the antichrist already in
the world and functioning through false teachers and
prophets. But Scripture says that there is a restraint on
his activity that will be removed just before the Lord's
coming: "When the thousand years are over, Satan will
be released from his prison" (Rev 20:7). While there will
always be a multitude of false teachers and prophets fulfilling the function of an antichrist, at a certain time the
unfettered power of Satan will concentrate its energies in a
single focus — perhaps in a single man — and operate without restraint.

Paul points this out to the Thessalonians, some of
whom had been disturbed by rumors or alleged prophe-

cies that the events preceding the Second Coming had already taken place. Paul calms the situation by showing that two important events that must precede the Lord's coming have not yet occurred: the mass apostasy and the manifestation of the "man of lawlessness". Here Paul is reminding his readers of truths that he had apparently already taught them during his previous visit with them:

> Let no one seduce you, no matter how. Since the mass apostasy has not yet occurred nor the man of lawlessness been revealed — that son of perdition and adversary who exalts himself above every so-called god proposed for worship, he who seats himself in God's temple and even declares himself to be God — do you not remember how I used to tell you about these things when I was still with you? You know what restrains him until he shall be revealed in his own time. The secret force of lawlessness is already at work, mind you, but there is one who holds him back until that restrainer shall be taken from the scene. Thereupon the lawless one will be revealed, and the Lord Jesus will destroy him with the breath of his mouth and annihilate him by manifesting his own presence. This lawless one will appear as part of the workings of Satan, accompanied by all the power and signs and wonders at the disposal of falsehood — by every seduction the wicked can devise for those destined to ruin because they have not opened their hearts to the truth in order to be saved (2 Th 2:3-10).

Paul says a great deal in these few verses. First of all, since he is simply reminding the Thessalonians of what he has already taught them concerning these truths, we can assume that they formed a regular part of his teaching.

Second, Paul indicates that lawlessness and hostility to God will be embodied in a person who is already at work but who is restrained at the moment from fully manifesting himself. Some Fathers of the Church thought the "restrainer" was the order imposed by the Roman Empire. Others have thought it to be the prayer of the Church, the preaching of the gospel, a divine decision, the Holy Spirit, or St. Michael the Archangel. While the exact identity of the restrainer is not indicated in the text, its reality and critical function is clearly taught.

Paul points out that the "man of lawlessness" will work to undermine men's knowledge of and loyalty to God and his truth; he will seek to put himself in the place of God, robbing God of the honor, fidelity, and obedience that are his due. Scripture indicates that there are two secret plans for mankind. God has one; its main outlines are now revealed to Christians, and it will culminate in the appearance, or parousia, of Christ. But Satan has a secret plan too; once the restrainer is removed, this plan will be seen clearly in another parousia, an appearing of embodied evil in the man of lawlessness. His coming will be accompanied by false signs and wonders and every seductive means that can be used to cause God's people to defect and be lost. In times of stress, human beings desperately look for a "savior". In such times the situation is ripe for a satanically "inspired" character or "savior figure" to appear on the scene. The Scriptures tell us as much as they do about the deception and false messiah of the last days precisely so Christians will be able to recognize and resist such deception.

I do not know whether the rapid removal of many restraints on the manifest working of evil in many of the Western countries in recent years is *the* removal of the restrainer and the prelude to the appearance of the antichrist. I do know that we are certainly living in a time where many of the Christian influences imbedded within the fabric of our society — its laws, customs, courts, governmental system, and schools — are being systematically stripped away. We are seeing the emergence of a new paganism that is openly hostile to God and his image in man, his ways, laws, and purposes. The Church in many parts of the world is already living through days of great tribulation.

Only after Satan finally manifests himself without restraint will Christ appear to destroy him and his works with his word, Spirit, and almighty presence.

As difficult as these times may be, Christians must bear in mind that Christ has won the victory and that those who bear his name and who have been willing to endure trials for his sake will share in his reward. We must also remember that he knows our strengths and weaknesses and will not let us be confronted with suffering that we cannot bear. "No test has been sent you that does not come to all men. Besides, God keeps his promise. He will not let you be tested beyond your strength. Along with the test he will give you a way out of it so that you may be able to endure it" (1 Cor 10:13). We can count on his great love, mercy, wisdom, and strength. St. Paul says in words we can make our own, "I consider the sufferings of the present to be as nothing compared with the glory to be revealed in us. Indeed, the whole created world eagerly awaits the revelation of the sons of God" (Rom 8:18–19). That glory to be revealed *in us,* that revelation of the sons of God in all their glory, will be unfolded in its fullness when Jesus returns.

The fundamental thing Christians contemplating the return of Christ should do is to live the kind of life that will enable them to "stand erect and hold your heads high, for your deliverance is at hand" (Lk 21:28). St. Peter tells us, "Set all your hope on the gift to be conferred on you when Jesus Christ appears" (1 Pet 1:13).

When Christ comes again, it will be to accomplish specific purposes. His coming will bring the resurrection of the dead and the judgment of all mankind. Let us now consider the resurrection that will accompany his coming.

SIX

The Resurrection of Christ and of Christians

On the third day he rose again in fulfilment of the Scriptures.

— Nicene Creed

The Resurrection is the manifestation of Christ's identity as Messiah, Savior, and Lord—a manifestation of his victory over death and of the reality of the redemption he has wrought.

But Christ's Resurrection is also for *us,* just as his suffering and death are for *us.* The fact that we share in his death through faith and baptism means that we also participate in his Resurrection. We share in Jesus' death and Resurrection in our initial faith and baptism, and our participation in these saving acts increases as we give ourselves more fully to God, dying more completely to "the old man" and to sin. When we ourselves are raised from the dead at Jesus' Second Coming, we will share fully in our inheritance as children of God.

To use Paul's terms, the Holy Spirit that we received

is a down payment or pledge on *our* resurrection. When Christ comes again, the promise guaranteed by that initial installment will be completely fulfilled.

Our Resurrection

Scripture refers to a certain order of events for the end of the age. First, it is when Christ comes again that we will be raised:

> Just as in Adam all die, so in Christ all will come to life again, but each one in proper order: Christ the first fruits and then, at his coming, all those who belong to him. After that will come the end (1 Cor 15:22–24).

Paul gives further information on the nature and order of these end-time events in his first letter to the church at Thessalonica:

> We would have you be clear about those who sleep in death, brothers; otherwise you might yield to grief like those who have no hope. For if we believe that Jesus died and rose, God will bring forth with him from the dead those also who have fallen asleep believing in him. We say to you, as if the Lord himself had said it, that we who live, who survive until his coming, will in no way have an advantage over those who have fallen asleep. No, the Lord himself will come down from heaven at the word of command, at the sound of the archangel's voice and God's trumpet; and those who have died in Christ will rise first.

Then we, the living, the survivors, will be caught up with them in the clouds to meet the Lord in the air. Thenceforth we shall be with the Lord unceasingly. Console one another with this message (1 Th 4:13–17).

First Christ is raised: the first fruits. This has already happened. And since the "first fruits" is plural, it may also refer to those who rose with Christ at the moment of his Resurrection — the first flowering or showing forth of what was to come for all:

Suddenly the curtain of the sanctuary was torn in two from top to bottom. The earth quaked, boulders split, tombs opened. Many bodies of saints who had fallen asleep were raised. After Jesus' resurrection they came forth from their tombs and entered the holy city and appeared to many (Mt 27:51–53).

Paul says that "those who have died in Christ will rise first" at Christ's coming and then goes out of his way to state solemnly, "as if the Lord himself had said it", that those Christians alive at Christ's coming will have no advantage over those who have already died. Rather, those who have *died in Christ,* dead Christians, will be raised first.

After these events, the living Christians, "all those who belong to him", will be caught up with the others "in the clouds to meet the Lord in the air". Some evangelical Protestants have referred to this event as "the rapture". It is not unreasonable to hold that this passage does not intend to describe the exact way living Christians will meet

Christ — that is, in the air and in the clouds. On the other hand, neither do I think it unreasonable to believe that the end will happen exactly as it is described. I am inclined to the latter view, because Paul is so specific in this text, because he speaks elsewhere about being caught up into heaven and shown special things by God (2 Cor 12:12), and because this passage is consistent with the specific parallels drawn by the angels between Jesus' Ascension and his return in glory: namely, "in a cloud", "into the heavens" (Acts 1:9–11).

This is the initial order of the resurrection: first Christ, the first fruits; then Christians who have died; then those Christians who are alive at Christ's Second Coming. Then will come the end.

Scripture seems to indicate clearly that the first sequence of events connected with the Second Coming of Christ will involve only Christians, both the dead and the living. This would make sense out of Gospel passages like the following, which we might otherwise find difficult to understand:

> So will it be at the coming of the Son of Man. Two men will be out in the field; one will be taken and one will be left. Two women will be grinding meal; one will be taken and one will be left. Stay awake, therefore! You cannot know the day your Lord is coming (Mt 24:39–42).[1]

---

[1] What *The Jerome Biblical Commentary* says about these verses is interesting: "The parousia will manifest the difference between men — a difference that is not now apparent. Two men plowing or two women grinding meal share the same occupation and look alike externally, but

If these and similar verses are read in light of 1 Corinthians 15:22–24 and 1 Thessalonians 4:13–17, a consistent picture emerges: the initial sequence of events at Christ's coming involves Christians.

Following the resurrection of Christians another sequence of events unfolds. This one involves the resurrection of all those not yet risen and the judgment of all mankind — including both those who died in their sins and the living wicked who were not caught up in the Lord.

Scripture clearly teaches this resurrection to judgment for reward or punishment, and it has been faithfully held by the Church in her creeds and teaching throughout the centuries.

We can see intimations of the final resurrection and judgment in the Old Testament.

At that time there shall arise
   Michael, the great prince,
guardian of your people;
It shall be a time unsurpassed in distress
   since nations began until that time.
At that time your people shall escape,
   everyone who is found written in the book.
Many of those who sleep
   in the dust of the earth shall awake;
some shall live forever,
   others shall be an everlasting horror and disgrace.

God knows the difference and will make it clear. The precise meaning of 'taken' and 'left' is not made clear, nor need it be" (*The Jerome Biblical Commentary* [Englewood Cliffs, N.J.: Prentice-Hall, 1968], 106).

But the wise shall shine brightly
   like the splendor of the firmament,
And those who lead the many to justice
   shall be like the stars forever.

(Dan 12:1–3)

Jesus confirms this truth:

The Father has given over to him power to pass
   judgment
because he is Son of Man;
no need for you to be surprised at this,
for an hour is coming
in which all those in their tombs
shall hear his voice and come forth.
Those who have done right shall rise to live;
the evildoers shall rise to be damned.

(Jn 5:27–29)

Paul points out that for all of us resurrection is a prelude to judgment. Because God takes our bodily nature seriously, we will be judged in the body for what we have done in the body: "The lives of all of us are to be revealed before the tribunal of Christ so that each one may receive his recompense, good or bad, according to his life in the body" (2 Cor 5:10).

Before discussing the judgment we will all face, let's consider in greater detail the significance of the resurrection.

The Significance of the Resurrection

Death is the greatest sign of man's fall from God's friendship. It is the most visible, overarching indicator that something has gone profoundly wrong with the human race. At its root, death is the curse that came upon the human race as a result of its rebellion against God:

> But by the envy of the devil, death entered the world,
> and they who are in his possession experience it.
>
> (Wis 2:24)

Scripture refers to death as "the last enemy" — the manifestation of man's fallenness most closely tied to the work of Satan and the last curse to yield to the power of redemption (1 Cor 15:26). Death will be destroyed, not in the first stages of redemption (when Satan will only be chained), but at Christ's Second Coming (when Satan will be thrown into the lake of fire to eternal ruin).

Because death is such an underlying torment to human life, casting a shadow over even its best moments, it lies at the heart of many of the fears and compulsions of the human race. In fact, the Epistle to the Hebrews talks of Jesus coming into the world to "free those who through fear of death had been slaves their whole life long" (Heb 2:15).

A key part of the significance of Christ's Resurrection for us, therefore, is that he frees us not only from death but from the *fear* of death. We will still die (unless we are alive when Christ returns), but Christians no longer need to fear death, because we know what awaits us — a glorious resurrection like Christ's. At his coming, death itself—personified in Satan and his helpers—will be eradicated. Perhaps Christ's words to his disciples that they would not see death (Jn 3:16) are best understood as referring to Death personified, as in Revelation 20:14 (the "angel of death" in certain Christian literature), or to the "second" and eternal death, the fate of the damned described in Revelation 2:11.

We are freed from the fear of death by joining ourselves to Christ in his death and Resurrection. We are given the Spirit to take away our fear and assure us of what awaits us at Jesus' coming. Living in the Spirit of Christ and filled with confidence in our coming resurrection, we can now live the new way of life to which Jesus calls his disciples; we can have those qualities that are characteristic of a life truly in Christ—freedom, confidence, trust, joy, peace, courage, fidelity, and strength to endure difficulty.

I cannot stress enough how important it is for us to *know* what awaits us because of Christ's Resurrection; this knowledge is a necessary precondition for living the way Jesus calls us to. He requires much of his disciples. We are able to give and do what our Master asks because of the power and hope released into our lives through knowledge of his Resurrection and faith for what we are to receive through it. For example, consider the following words of Jesus to his disciples:

> It is not for you to be in search of what you are to eat or drink. Stop worrying. The unbelievers of this world are always running after these things. Your Father knows that you need such things. Seek out in-

stead his kingship over you, and the rest will follow in turn (Lk 12:29-31).

The characteristic feature of unbelievers, whether they are rich or poor, is anxiety over material possessions and the basics of life. Their insecurity about impoverishment and possible bodily harm to themselves and their loved ones is, at root, a fear of death.

But Jesus clearly indicates that those who believe in him — in the power of his death and Resurrection and in the authority made manifest in his Resurrection — should have an entirely different perspective on life: they should experience trust and confidence that God will provide as his followers seek to put him first in all things. This attitude of trust is impossible without that freedom from the fear of death that comes by partaking in and beholding the victory won in the Resurrection of Christ. For now, this triumph over death is attested to us by the Holy Spirit in a preliminary way, but at the Second Coming we shall taste it in its fullness.

Jesus specifically counsels his followers to fear only one thing — the possibility of going to hell:

> I say to you who are my friends: Do not be afraid of those who kill the body and can do no more. I will show you whom you ought to fear. Fear him who has power to cast into Gehenna after he has killed. Yes, I tell you, fear him (Lk 12:4-5).

"To know Christ and the power flowing from his resurrection" was Paul's desire (Phil 3:10). This freed him from the fear of death and allowed him to help his fellow

Christians to be likewise free and to exclaim with him: "O death, where is your victory? O death, where is your sting?" (1 Cor 15:55).

The Resurrection of Christ is central to the Christian faith. The Church has always regarded it as one of the fundamental truths of the faith, a foundation stone that she has guarded through the centuries against all attacks. Christ's Resurrection is a sign of his identity as Savior and Lord; it is our assurance that his sacrifice was accepted by the Father, that his words are true, and that we can rely on him as the Just One appointed by God. The Resurrection of Christ signals the conquering of death, the lifting of the curse, the crushing of Satan, the redemption of our race. It is a sign that God has truly entered into our race and into combat with our enemy. It guarantees that he has saved us as he created us — as flesh-and-blood creatures, redeemed through a flesh-and-blood Savior who was raised victorious from the dead in his body as a sign of the salvation of the material world.

Attempts to obscure Christ and these saving actions are attempts to obscure the truth. Blocking access to this person and these events deprives man of his sole means to God, freedom, forgiveness of sins, life in the Spirit, and resurrection.

These attempts appeared early in the Church, and Paul vigorously resisted them:

> Tell me, if Christ is preached as raised from the dead, how is it that some of you say there is no resurrection of the dead? If there is no resurrection of the dead, Christ himself has not been raised. And if Christ has

not been raised, our preaching is void of content and your faith is empty too. Indeed, we should then be exposed as false witnesses of God, for we have borne witness before him that he raised up Christ; but he certainly did not raise him up if the dead are not raised. Why? Because if the dead are not raised, your faith is worthless. You are still in your sins, and those who have fallen asleep in Christ are the deadest of the dead. If our hopes in Christ are limited to this life only, we are the most pitiable of men.

But as it is, Christ is now raised from the dead, the first fruits of those who have fallen asleep (1 Cor 15:12–20).

Today, as in Paul's time, there are those even within the Christian church who are undermining fundamental truths of the faith, including the Resurrection. There are theologians today who are in effect denying the reality of the Resurrection of Christ by talking about it, not as an actual event, but simply as a psychological awareness of the early disciples about the enduring meaning and significance of Jesus for coming generations.[2] This contradicts

---

[2] Concern for this watering down of scriptural teaching in these areas has led the Catholic Church to issue an alert to her bishops in this regard: "Those responsible in this matter must be extremely attentive to anything that might introduce into the general attitude of the faithful a gradual debasement or progressive extinction of any element of the baptismal creed necessary for the coherence of the faith and inseparably connected with important practices in the life of the Church.

"We think it urgently necessary to call one of these elements to the attention of those to whom God has entrusted the function of advancing and protecting the faith, in order that they may forestall the dangers that could threaten this faith in the minds of the faithful.

the fact that Jesus really rose from the dead and was actually seen and touched by the disciples and that he demonstrated a resurrected body that was also to be theirs.

As we think about the glorious truth of Christ's Resurrection and ours, certain questions come to mind. We will consider two of them now.

What Happens after Death and before Resurrection?

The teaching of Scripture is clear that the resurrection of human beings will occur at the Second Coming of Christ.

"The element in question is the article of the Creed concerning life everlasting and so everything in general after death. When setting forth this teaching, it is not permissible to remove any point, nor can a defective or uncertain outlook be adopted without endangering the faith and salvation of Christians.

"The importance of this final article of the baptismal Creed is obvious: it expresses the goal and purpose of God's plan, the unfolding of which is described in the Creed. If there is no resurrection, the whole structure of faith collapses, as Saint Paul states so forcefully (cf. 1 Cor 15). If the content of the words 'life everlasting' is uncertain for Christians, the promises contained in the Gospel and the meaning of creation and redemption disappear, and even earthly life must be said to be deprived of all hope (cf. Heb 11:1). . . . The Church believes in the resurrection of the dead. . . . The Church understands this resurrection as referring to *the whole person*; for the elect it is nothing other than the extension to human beings of the Resurrection of Christ itself" (*The Reality of Life after Death* from the Congregation for the Doctrine of the Faith, issued May 11, 1979, with the approval of Pope John Paul II, reprinted in Austin Flannery, *Vatican Council II*, vol. 2: *More Post Conciliar Documents* [Boston: Daughters of St. Paul, 1982], 500–501).

What happens then after death to those who die before the Second Coming? Scripture mentions "the sleep of death" (1 Th 4:13), but this does not provide much insight into what the actual state is like. In other places though, almost inadvertently, we are given insights and glimpses into the nature of life after death and before the resurrection.

Scripture distinguishes between the life of the body and the life of the soul or spirit, which continues after our bodily death. Jesus warns us not to fear those who can kill the body but rather him who also has power to kill the soul (Mt 10:28). Stephen, at the point of death, prays, "Lord Jesus, receive my spirit" (Acts 7:59).

Other Scripture passages suggest that some kind of participation in the life of the blessed or the life of the damned begins immediately after death, even before the resurrection of the body. The story of Dives and Lazarus presents Lazarus as participating in the life of the blessed immediately after death and Dives in the torment of the damned; they remain within sight and communication of each other, yet with a great abyss between them (Lk 16:19–31). On the Cross, Jesus promised the believing thief that "this day, you will be with me in paradise" (Lk 23:42).

This understanding of life after death before the resurrection is further clarified by the following passage from the First Epistle of Peter. After Christ died, he descended into Hades (what the Apostles' Creed states as "he descended into hell") to proclaim his saving work to the imprisoned spirits:

The reason why Christ died for sins once for all, the just man for the sake of the unjust, was that he might lead you to God. He was put to death insofar as fleshly existence goes, but was given life in the realm of the spirit. It was in the spirit also that he went to preach to the spirits in prison (1 Pet 3:18–19).

Over the years, significant Church bodies have affirmed the reliability of these glimpses from Scripture and have incorporated them into their teaching. This teaching maintains that the soul or spirit of a person already begins to participate in his eternal destiny after death and that the complete form of reward or punishment awaits the resurrection of the body and the final judgment accompanying the Second Coming of Christ.[3]

One last question about the resurrection before we consider the nature of the final judgment: What kind of resurrected bodies will we have?

---

[3] In order to counter modern efforts to undermine these truths, "The Church affirms that a spiritual element survives and subsists after death, an element endowed with consciousness and will, so that the 'human self' subsists. To designate this element, the Church uses the word 'soul', the accepted term in the usage of Scripture and Tradition. Although not unaware that this term has various meanings in the Bible, the Church thinks that there is no valid reason for rejecting it; moreover, she considers that the use of some word as a vehicle is absolutely indispensable in order to support the faith of Christians. . . . In accordance with the Scriptures, the Church looks for 'the glorious manifestation of our Lord, Jesus Christ' (*Dei Verbum*, 1, 4), believing it to be distinct and deferred with respect to the situation of people immediately after death" (C.D.F. *The Reality of Life after Death*, p. 502 in Flannery).

What Will Our Resurrected Bodies Be Like?

As with many other questions, Scripture does not tell us all we might like to know about this but just what we need to know. The main scriptural teaching on the resurrected body is in 1 Corinthians 15:35–54. Here Paul makes two basic points. The first is that there is some similarity between the earthly body and the resurrected body. (Paul compares it to the relationship between the seed and the full-grown plant.) The second point is that this real continuity does not exclude a real discontinuity between the earthly body and the resurrected body, since the resurrection brings us into a different order of existence where many of earth's natural laws no longer obtain. In order to give some idea of the difference between the earthly body and the resurrected body, Paul contrasts Adam and Christ:

> The first man was of earth, formed from dust, the second is from heaven. Just as we resemble the man from earth, so shall we bear the likeness of the man from heaven (1 Cor 15:47–49).

Paul indicates that our resurrected bodies will be incorruptible, glorious, and immortal.

We can see the interplay of continuity and discontinuity, earthly and heavenly, in the accounts about the resurrected Christ. Prior to his Resurrection, Christ was bound by the limits of his earthly body and was subject to the laws of space and time, generation and decay. After his Resurrection he was still corporeal: he had a tangible body that could be touched and felt, that could eat, that his disciples could experience as solid and real, that still bore the marks of his wounds, that was recognizable as the Jesus they had known and lived with for three years. Yet at the same time, Jesus had been transformed by the Resurrection, and his disciples often did not recognize him. His resurrected body could transcend the limitations and physical laws to which his earthly body had been subject: he could now enter locked rooms, appear and disappear.

Jesus' Resurrection is a model for ours; his resurrected body prefigures what ours will be like. We will be the same as before in some respects, yet different; corporeal, but not bound in the same way by space and time; human, but now also incorruptible, immortal, glorious. As Paul writes:

> Now I am going to tell you a mystery. Not all of us shall fall asleep, but all of us are to be changed — in an instant, in the twinkling of an eye, at the sound of the last trumpet. The trumpet will sound and the dead will be raised incorruptible, and we shall be changed. This corruptible body must be clothed with incorruptibility, this mortal body with immortality. When the corruptible frame takes on incorruptibility and the mortal immortality, then will the saying of scripture be fulfilled (1 Cor 15:51–54).

Whether the actual atoms and molecules from our earthly bodies, dissolved in their graves, will be used in our resurrected bodies is just one of those questions that Scripture does not answer. Questions like this seem irrelevant, especially now that we know that the matter in our bodies is continually being replaced and that by the time we die our body will contain no matter present in our body at birth. Yet we have been told clearly what we need to know: we shall be raised with him, incorruptible, immortal, glorious.[4]

Christ will come again. At his coming the righteous and the wicked will be raised, and then will come the judgment. Now let us turn to a consideration of the judgment.

---

[4] As John Paul II has reaffirmed regarding matters and questions like this: "Neither Scripture nor theology provides sufficient light for a proper picture of life after death. Christians must firmly hold the two following points essential: On the one hand they must believe in the fundamental continuity, thanks to the power of the Holy Spirit, between our present life in Christ and the future life . . . ; on the other hand they must be clearly aware of the radical break between the present life and the future one, due to the fact that the economy of faith will be replaced by the economy of fullness of life: We shall be with Christ and 'we shall see God' (cf. 1 Jn 3:2), and it is in these promises and marvelous mysteries that our hope essentially consists. Our imagination may be incapable of reaching these heights, but our heart does so instinctively and completely" (ibid.).

SEVEN

The Final Judgment

The final judgment is another of the central themes of the Bible and a great foundational truth of the Christian faith.

Justice is never done perfectly here on earth: the good die young; the righteous suffer; the poor are defrauded. But God's word speaks over and over of that great Day of Yahweh, when God's faithful ones will be rewarded and blessed beyond measure, when God's enemies and those who have lived unrighteous lives will be definitively punished.

The coming reign of God's anointed messiah-king, along with the certain hope that at his coming all things will be set right, is prophesied again and again by the Old Testament prophets.

The reign of God was inaugurated with the life, suffering, death, Resurrection, and Ascension of Jesus and the sending of the Spirit; with these, the age of the Church began. But the reign of God will not be fully established until the age of the Church is brought to a conclusion, along with all of human history, at the Second Coming of Jesus. Jesus' First Coming was as a sacrificial lamb, as an offering for our sin; his Second Coming will be as a judge, to render a verdict about how each human being and all of human history responded to his First Coming. As the Creed states: "He will come again to judge the living and the dead, and of his kingdom there will be no end."

This Day of Yahweh, this consummation of human history, this Second Coming of the Lord Jesus, will be a day of joy and exultation for God's faithful ones but a day of terror for his enemies. The preaching of the entire New Testament occurs against the backdrop of the certainty and centrality of this coming judgment of human life and history.

John the Baptist prepared the way for Jesus by proclaiming repentance in the face of the coming judgment, "the wrath to come". His proclamation of the coming of Jesus is also an announcement of the judgment and wrath that will follow the completion of Jesus' mission:

> When he saw that many of the Pharisees and Sadducees were stepping forward for this bath, he said to them: "You brood of vipers! Who told you to flee from the wrath to come? Give some evidence that you mean to reform. . . . Even now the ax is laid to the root of the tree. Every tree that is not fruitful will be cut down and thrown into the fire. I baptize you in water for the sake of reform, but the one who will follow me is more powerful than I. I am not even fit to carry his sandals. He it is who will baptize you in the Holy Spirit and fire. His winnowing-fan is in his hand. He will clear the threshing floor and gather

his grain into the barn, but the chaff he will burn in unquenchable fire" (Mt 3:7–8, 10–12).

Jesus has come, declares John the Baptist, to bestow the Spirit on those who repent and to decree eternal judgment for those who refuse. It is clear that Jesus saw his mission in the light of the impending judgment; he saw himself as calling people to a repentance and faith in him that would allow them to escape condemnation on the last day.

When entire regions or towns rejected Jesus' message, he did not hesitate to warn of the severity of the punishment to be pronounced on them at the day of judgment. To the nonresponsive Galilean cities that ignored his miracles, Jesus said: "I assure you, it will go easier for Tyre and Sidon than for you on the day of judgment. . . . It will go easier for Sodom than for you on the day of judgment" (Mt 11:22, 24). Concerning those who reject his representatives: "If anyone does not receive you or listen to what you have to say, leave that house or town, and once outside it shake its dust from your feet. I assure you, it will go easier for the region of Sodom and Gomorrah on the day of judgment than it will for that town" (Mt 10:14–15).

Along with these classic examples of God's previous judgments, Jesus also counseled his hearers to view current catastrophes — like a tower falling and killing eighteen people — as warnings from God to repent and escape the coming judgment (Lk 13:4). Whether directly willed by God (like the destruction of Sodom and Gomorrah), or whether apparently "chance" occurrences (like the collapse of the tower), Jesus sees the catastrophes of human history as forewarnings sent or permitted by God to encourage repentance.

The New Testament continually restates this basic teaching about the coming judgment.

The preaching of Acts:

> God may well have overlooked bygone periods when men did not know him; but now he calls on all men everywhere to reform their lives. He has set the day on which he is going to "judge the world with justice" through a man he has appointed—one whom he has endorsed in the sight of all by raising him from the dead (Acts 17:30–31).

Paul to the Romans:

> We shall all have to appear before the judgment seat of God. . . . Every one of us will have to give an account of himself before God (Rom 14:10, 12).

Peter to the diaspora:

> They shall give an accounting to him who stands ready to judge the living and the dead (1 Pet 4:5).

> The present heavens and earth are reserved by God's word for fire; they are kept for the day of judgment, the day when godless men will be destroyed (2 Pet 3:7).

John, in Revelation:

> The dead were judged according to their conduct as recorded on the scrolls. The sea gave up its dead; then death and the nether world gave up their dead.

Each person was judged according to his conduct (Rev 20:12–13).

From this it is clear that the very message of salvation is presented in connection with the coming judgment. The salvation offered by Jesus is salvation from the wrath to come, from condemnation on the day of judgment.

The people of those parts are reporting what kind of reception we had from you, and how you turned to God from idols, to serve him who is the living and true God and to await from heaven the Son he raised from the dead—Jesus, who delivers us from the wrath to come (1 Th 1:9–10).

Now that we have been justified by his blood, it is all the more certain that we shall be saved by him from God's wrath (Rom 5:9).

The message of Scripture is clear: God is merciful and just. He extends his mercy now through his Son Jesus Christ, who died and rose for our salvation. But this age of mercy and grace will come to an end; those who have rejected God's offer of grace and mercy will experience his wrath. God is just as well as merciful. Those who choose not to enter his kingdom through Jesus, the doorway he has established, are left outside forever:

Consider the kindness and severity of God—severity toward those who fell, kindness toward you, provided you remain in his kindness; if you do not, you too will be cut off (Rom 11:22).

Now let us consider what Scripture tells us about the basis for God's judgment.

The Basis of Judgment for Christians

For Christians who have believed in Christ and obeyed him, the day of judgment is the long-awaited day of fullness of redemption and reward. Scripture encourages those Christians who have been living in union with and obedience to Christ to approach the day of judgment with confidence and joyful expectation. For Christians, the Lord's coming and his judgment are fundamentally events of vindication and fulfillment. In fact, as we have seen, Peter urges Christians to "set all your hope on the gift to be conferred on you when Jesus Christ appears" (1 Pet 1:13), and Luke, in speaking of the events leading up to the Second Coming and judgment, says, "When you see these things, look up in joy, your deliverance is at hand" (Lk 21:28).

Paul declares that "there is no condemnation now for those who are in Christ Jesus" and goes on to specify why: "If the Spirit of him who raised Jesus from the dead dwells in you, then he who raised Christ from the dead will bring your mortal bodies to life also, through his Spirit dwelling in you" (Rom 8:1, 11). Paul then adds that when Christ comes, we will see that the sufferings of the present are nothing compared with the glory to be revealed in us. Indeed, he says, "the whole created world eagerly awaits the revelation of the sons of God", and "we ourselves, although we have the Spirit as first fruits, groan

inwardly while we await the redemption of our bodies"
(vv. 19, 23).

John, too, reassures those who are following the Lord:

Whoever believes in him avoids condemnation,
but whoever does not believe is already
   condemned.

(Jn 3:18)

I solemnly assure you,
the man who hears my word
and has faith in him who sent me
possesses eternal life.
He does not come under condemnation,
but has passed from death to life.
I solemnly assure you,
an hour is coming, has indeed come,
when the dead shall hear the voice of the Son of God,
and those who have heeded it shall live. . . .
an hour is coming
in which all those in their tombs
shall hear his voice and come forth.
Those who have done right shall rise to live;
the evildoers shall rise to be damned.

(Jn 5:24–25, 28–29)

Our love is brought to perfection in this,
that we should have confidence on the day of
   judgment;
for our relation to this world is just like his.

(1 Jn 4:17)

Christians who believe in Christ and obey him, and are therefore living in the same relation to the world as Jesus did and does, should have confidence on the day of judgment.

At the same time, though, Christians too will have to give an account of their lives. Things that have not been set right or corrected adequately before Christ's coming will be dealt with. However, the Christians being judged will know — the Lord having affirmed it — that they are saved and have escaped from wrath and condemnation. In other words, their judgment will be in terms of correction and purification, not condemnation, and will issue ultimately in reward.

Among those things for which no reward will be given, Jesus mentions religious activities done with impure motives (for example, to appear good or holy to others). Almsgiving, prayer, and fasting to impress others are particularly singled out (Mt 6:1–18). What has been hidden will be brought into the light:

> Stop passing judgment before the time of his return. He will bring to light what is hidden in darkness and manifest the intentions of hearts. At that time, everyone will receive his praise from God (1 Cor 4:5).

Anything in our life and work that has not really been built solidly on Christ and in harmony with his intentions will be judged. Although these things may be found lacking, we ourselves will be saved:

> Thanks to the favor God showed me I laid a foundation as a wise master-builder might do, and now

someone else is building upon it. Everyone, however, must be careful how he builds. No one can lay a foundation other than the one that has been laid, namely Jesus Christ. If different ones build on this foundation with gold, silver, precious stones, wood, hay or straw, the work of each will be made clear. The Day will disclose it. That day will make its appearance with fire, and fire will test the quality of each man's work. If the building a man has raised on this foundation still stands, he will receive his recompense. If a man's building burns, he will suffer loss. He himself will be saved, but only as one fleeing through fire. (1 Cor 3:10–15).

The Catholic understanding of purgatory is related to Scriptures like these, which indicate the need for a purification by "fire" for those who are not to be condemned but are in need of some purification before being able to enter fully into the heavenly presence of God.[1] Popular understandings of purgatory have generally emphasized the negative aspects of the pain of purification, while perhaps not bringing out clearly enough that to be in purgatory is to be assured of heaven, to be saved, and is already a source of profound joy. John Paul II has brought out this positive dimension in his teaching:

One further point should be made: life's earthly journey has an end which, if a person reaches it in friendship with God, coincides with the first moment of eternal bliss. Even, if in that passage to heaven, the soul must undergo the purification of the last impu-

[1] CCC, 1030–32.

rities through purgatory, it is already filled with light, certitude and joy, because the person knows that he belongs forever to God.[2]

Saint Catherine of Genoa's treatise on purgatory brings out this positive dimension quite well:

I believe no happiness can be found worthy to be compared with that of a soul in Purgatory except that of the saints in Paradise. And day by day this happiness grows as God flows into these souls, more and more as the hindrance to His entrance is consumed. Sin's rust is the hindrance, and the fire burns the rust away so that more and more the soul opens itself up to the divine inflowing.[3]

Part of the judgment for Christians will be a determining of reward. Apparently, there are degrees of reward and glory in heaven, related to the degree of love and service with which we have followed Christ. For example, those who turn others to righteousness will be especially blessed (Dan 12:3).

Judgment on Lukewarm Christians

This may come as something of a surprise, but Scripture indicates that lukewarm Christians have a chance of be-

[2] John Paul II, "The Holy Spirit and Hope", *L'Osservatore Romano*, English language ed., July 8, 1991.

[3] This treatise of St. Catherine of Genoa has been published under the title *Fire of Love: Understanding Purgatory,* (Manchester, N.H.: Sophia Institute Press, 1996).

ing damned. I was surprised, even shocked, when I studied what God's word said about this. The general tone of preaching, religious education, and theology today convey the impression that damnation is not a serious possibility for the average lukewarm Christian. God's word points in a quite different direction.

Jesus' general attitude toward lukewarmness is vividly expressed in the following excerpt from Revelation:

> I know your deeds: I know you are neither hot nor cold. How I wish you were one or the other — hot or cold! But because you are lukewarm, neither hot nor cold, I will spew you out of my mouth! (Rev 3:15).

The prophet Malachi speaks of judgment as a day when "you will again see the distinction between . . . him who serves God, and him who does not serve him" (Malachi 3:18). And the New Testament makes clear that saving faith is not just intellectual assent to certain truths, or even an emotional "born-again" experience, but a commitment of the heart and will to act on and live in accordance with the words that our Savior and Lord speaks to us, in the power of the Holy Spirit. "Be assured, then, that faith without works is dead as a body without breath" (James 2:26).

To profess faith in Christ without the corresponding action is counted by Jesus as worthy of condemnation:

> Every tree that does not bear good fruit is cut down and thrown into the fire. You can tell a tree by its fruit. None of those who cry out, "Lord, Lord," will

enter the kingdom of God but only the one who
does the will of my Father in heaven. When that day
comes, many will plead with me, "Lord, Lord". . . .
Then I will declare to them solemnly, "I never knew
you. Out of my sight, you evildoers!" (Mt 7:19–22,
23).

Likewise to believe in the Lord but not to profess
that faith before others when necessary is to be liable to
damnation:

I tell you, whoever acknowledges me before men —
the Son of Man will acknowledge him before the angels of God. But the man who has disowned me in
the presence of men will be disowned in the presence
of the angels of God (Lk 12:8–9).

Not to be fruitful for the Lord, not to use well what he
gives, is to run the risk of condemnation. Material possessions, gifts and abilities, time and resources, insights and
faith — an unprofitable use of any of these things could
result in their being taken away and their "owners" being
declared unfaithful servants. This is what is indicated in
the parable of the silver pieces or talents. The servant who
has not made a profit with the master's money is stripped
of the talents he was given and thrown out into the outer
darkness:

Take the thousand away from him and give it to the
man with the ten thousand. Those who have, will get
more until they grow rich, while those who have not,
will lose even the little they have. Throw this worth-

less servant into the darkness outside, where he can wail and grind his teeth (Mt 25:28–30).[4]

Scripture also points out the dangers of becoming so involved in ordinary life that one is not living alert to God, eager to do Christ's will and ready for Christ's Second Coming:

> The coming of the Son of Man will repeat what happened in Noah's time. In the days before the flood people were eating and drinking, marrying and being married, right up to the day Noah entered the ark. They were totally unconcerned until the flood came and destroyed them. So will it be at the coming of the Son of Man (Mt 24:37–39).[5]

To be nominal Christians but not to be clothed in righteous deeds makes one unfit for the kingdom of God. Being invited into the kingdom is one thing; responding properly is another:

> When the king came in to meet the guests, however, he caught sight of a man not properly dressed for a

[4] Remarking on this passage, *The Jerome Biblical Commentary* states: "This paradoxical saying indicates that the powers conferred on the disciples grow with use and wither with disuse. The punishment for this type of infidelity is as severe as the punishment for more positive sins; it is expulsion into outer darkness" (*The Jerome Biblical Commentary* [Englewood Cliffs, N.J.: Prentice-Hall, 1968], 106).

[5] Again, the explanations of *The Jerome Biblical Commentary* are helpful: "The warning about the deluge is significant; it does not say that men were sinning but that they were engaged in innocent secular occupations. Their sin was to give no thought to impending catastrophe. The disciples are warned against that interest in secular business that makes them forget the parousia" (ibid.).

wedding feast. "My friend," he said, "how is it you came in here not properly dressed?" The man had nothing to say. The king then said to the attendants, "Bind him hand and foot and throw him out into the night to wail and grind his teeth." The invited are many, the elect are few (Mt 22:11–14).

We also become liable to judgment if we fail to persevere in faith and obedience until the end of our lives or until the Lord's return. Short-lived enthusiasm followed by a drifting back into lukewarmness means possible condemnation:

Happy that servant whom his master discovers at work on his return! I assure you, he will put him in charge of all his property. But if the servant is worthless and tells himself, "My master is a long time in coming," and begins to beat his fellow servants, to eat and drink with drunkards, that man's master will return when he is not ready and least expects him. He will punish him severely and settle with him as is done with hypocrites. There will be wailing then and grinding of teeth (Mt 24:46–51).

Being faithful to the end is essential for salvation:

Remain faithful until death and I will give you the crown of life. . . . [H]old fast to what you have until I come.

To the one who wins the victory, who keeps to my ways till the end, I will give authority over the nations — the same authority I received from my Father (Rev 2:10, 25, 26).

Christians who do not persevere, who end up denying the faith and leading others to do likewise, will be dealt with severely:

> Just as weeds are collected and burned, so will it be at the end of the world. The Son of Man will dispatch his angels to collect from his kingdom all who draw others to apostasy, and all evildoers. The angels will hurl them into the fiery furnace where they will wail and grind their teeth. Then the saints will shine like the sun in their Father's kingdom. Let everyone heed what he hears! (Mt 13:40–43).

Returning to serious sin after being a Christian puts us in risk of judgment.

> If we sin willfully after receiving the truth, there remains for us no further sacrifice for sin — only a fearful expectation of judgment and a flaming fire to consume the adversaries of God. Anyone who rejects the law of Moses is put to death without mercy on the testimony of two or three witnesses. Do you not suppose that a much worse punishment is due the man who disdains the Son of God, thinks the covenant-blood by which he was sanctified to be ordinary, and insults the Spirit of grace? We know who said, "Vengeance is mine; I will repay" and "The Lord will judge his people." It is a fearful thing to fall into the hands of the living God (Heb 10:26–31).

There is only one way for Christians to meet the criteria required for heaven: by God's grace and our response in faith we must allow the Lord to transform us and make us holy—not just in external actions, but in our hearts and minds and wills, for "unless your holiness surpasses that of the scribes and Pharisees you shall not enter the kingdom of God" (Mt 5:20).

The Judgment of Those Who Hear the Gospel but Reject It

Human beings who hear the gospel and encounter its messengers but close their hearts to it will be condemned:

> He will provide relief to you who are sorely tried, as well as to us, when the Lord Jesus is revealed from heaven with his mighty angels; when "with flaming power he will inflict punishment on those who do not acknowledge God nor heed" the good news of our Lord Jesus. Such as these will suffer the penalty of eternal ruin apart from the presence of the Lord and the glory of his might on the Day when he comes, to be glorified in his holy ones and adored by all who have believed—for you already have our witness to you (2 Th 1:7–10).

Numerous other passages speak of condemnation as the consequence for rejecting the gospel. We have considered some of these already; we shall consider others later. Regarding the reception accorded to messengers of the gospel, Jesus himself promises that those who reject his brethren will be judged as if they had rejected him:

> If anyone does not receive you or listen to what you have to say, leave that house or town, and once out-

side it shake its dust from your feet. I assure you, it will go easier for the region of Sodom and Gomorrah on the day of judgment than it will for that town.

He who welcomes you welcomes me, and he who welcomes me welcomes him who sent me. He who welcomes a prophet because he bears the name of prophet receives a prophet's reward; he who welcomes a holy man because he is known to be holy receives a holy man's reward. And I promise you that whoever gives a cup of cold water to one of these lowly ones because he is a disciple will not want for his reward (Mt 10:14–15, 40–42).

Reward and punishment for the treatment of Jesus' disciples are both amplified in the judgment scene from Matthew:

"I assure you, as often as you did it for one of my least brothers, you did it for me."
Then he will say to those on his left: "Out of my sight, you condemned, into that everlasting fire prepared for the devil and his angels! . . . I assure you, as often as you neglected to do it to one of these least ones, you neglected to do it to me." These will go off to eternal punishment and the just to eternal life (Mt 25:40–41, 45–46).

In the New Testament, the word "brethren" always refers to fellow Christians. Thus this judgment scene describes the consequences of how Christ's disciples, his brothers, are treated. (This is not to deny that Christians are also called to be "good Samaritans", compassionate

and merciful to all men. This too will affect the judgment
[Lk 10:30–37; Mt 5:43–48].)

Scripture also specifies certain types of behavior that
will exclude their practitioners from the kingdom of God,
should they die unrepentant. Among those barred from
heaven will be those who dishonor marriage; those who
live as thieves, idolaters, sodomites, misers, fornicators,
adulterers, drunkards, slanderers, robbers; those who are
liars or who do detestable acts; those who are cowards,
traitors, deceivers (Heb 13:4; 1 Cor 6:9–11; Rev 21:8,
26–27). God alone can judge hearts, and "although we
can judge that an act is in itself a grave offense, we must
entrust judgment of persons to the justice and mercy of
God (CCC 1861).

In addition, false teachers — especially those who deny
the Lord, his Second Coming, or the judgment, or who
encourage immorality — will be excluded from the kingdom. Even the fallen angels will receive a final judgment
and be eternally banished from it (2 Pet 2:1–22, 3:1–4).

The Judgment of Those Who
Have Not Heard the Gospel

Scripture indicates that human beings who have not heard
the gospel before their deaths or the Lord's coming will be
judged on the basis of their response to the light that God
gave them. God gives this light, or revelation, of himself
at least minimally to all mankind through the material
creation. It also manifests itself in that call to a moral life

that God gives to all men — the instinct, sense of right and wrong, or conscience implanted in each of us:

> The wrath of God is being revealed from heaven against the irreligious and perverse spirit of men who, in this perversity of theirs, hinder the truth. In fact, whatever can be known about God is clear to them; he himself made it so. Since the creation of the world, invisible realities, God's eternal power and divinity, have become visible, recognized through the things he has made. Therefore these men are inexcusable. They certainly had knowledge of God, yet they did not glorify him as God or give him thanks; they stultified themselves through speculating to no purpose, and their senseless hearts were darkened. . . . They know God's just decree that all who do such things deserve death; yet they not only do them but approve them in others (Rom 1:18–21, 32).

Concerning the instinct for right and wrong in all men:

> Sinners who do not have the law will perish without reference to it; sinners bound by the law will be judged in accordance with it. For it is not those who hear the law who are just in the sight of God; it is those who keep it who will be declared just. When Gentiles who do not have the law keep it as by instinct, these men although without the law serve as a law for themselves. They show that the demands of the law are written in their hearts. Their conscience bears witness together with that law, and their thoughts will accuse or defend them on the day

when, in accordance with the gospel I preach, God will pass judgment on the secrets of men through Christ Jesus (Rom 2:12–16).

The Second Vatican Council gives a good presentation of this scriptural teaching about the possible salvation of those who have not heard the gospel. The Council document *Lumen Gentium* affirms God's closeness to and desire to save all men:

> Nor is God Himself far distant from those who in shadows and images seek the unknown God, for it is He who gives to all men life and breath and every other gift (cf. Acts 17:25–28), and who as Savior wills that all men be saved (cf. 1 Tim 2:4) (Constitution on the Church, 16).

It then points out the scriptural revelation about how people in this situation will be judged and how salvation is possible for them:

> Those also can attain to everlasting salvation who through no fault of their own do not know the gospel of Christ or His Church, yet sincerely seek God and, moved by grace, strive by their deeds to do His Will as it is known to them through the dictates of conscience. Nor does divine Providence deny the help necessary for salvation to those who without blame on their part have not yet arrived at an explicit knowledge of God but who strive to live a good life, thanks to His grace. Whatever goodness or truth is found among them is looked upon by the Church as a preparation for the gospel. She regards such quali-

ties as given by Him who enlightens all men so that they may finally have life.

Note here the qualifications placed on the possibility for salvation. First, those ignorant of the gospel are saved only by grace given by God, as a result of the sacrifice of Christ. Also, these people must be ignorant of the gospel "through no fault of their own", and they must be people who "sincerely seek God" and who "strive . . . to do His Will as it is known to them".

Recognizing that such people may be comparatively rare and that the fallen human race does not often fulfill the mentioned conditions, the Council document goes on to point out realistically the actual situation:

> But rather often men, deceived by the Evil One, have become caught up in futile reasoning and have exchanged the truth of God for a lie, serving the creature rather than the Creator (cf. Rom 1:21, 25). Or some there are who, living and dying in a world without God, are subject to utter hopelessness. Consequently, to promote the glory of God and procure the salvation of all such men, and mindful of the command of the Lord, "Preach the gospel to every creature" (Mk 16:16), the Church painstakingly fosters her missionary work.

The fact is that it is infinitely preferable for human beings to be found "in Christ" on the day of judgment rather than to presume that fallen humanity is sincerely and actively seeking God and his will. So often men are "deceived by the Evil One" and end up worshipping the creature rather than the Creator. Therefore, to preach the gospel to every creature is not just an optional extra, or even simply a duty out of obedience, but it is an act of great mercy to fallen mankind.

The Consequences of Judgment: Hell and Heaven

With the Second Coming of Christ, the resurrection of the dead, and the final judgment, human history as we currently know it will come to an end. The time of mercy will draw to a close for those in rebellion against God, and along with it the chance to escape his wrath and punishment. Evildoers will be banished from his kingdom forever and enter into eternal punishment. Those who have responded to the light God gave them will enter into eternal joy.

Hell, the fate of the damned, is vividly described in Scripture.[6] Sometimes it is referred to as "outer darkness" (Mt 22:13), where there will be weeping and gnashing of teeth. Sometimes it is described as "unquenchable fire" (Mk 9:43), or the "furnace of fire" (Mt 13:42, 50), or the "lake of fire" (Rev 20:15; 21:8). Sometimes, it is the place where the tormenting worm never stops gnawing (Mk 9:48). Sometimes it is simply "damnation" or "death" (Jn 5:25, 29), the "second death" (Rev 2:11, 20:14), "eternal punishment" (Mt 25:46), or "eternal ruin" (2 Th 1:7–10).

The reality of the scriptural teaching on hell gives rise to a number of questions—most immediately, perhaps, concerning the images used to describe it. Will hell liter-

---

[6] CCC, 1033–37.

ally be a place of flames, darkness, and tormenting worms? Perhaps. Perhaps not. The only certainty is that Scripture warns us to do everything possible to avoid ending up there, since its sufferings are truly awful. But at the same time, we are overstepping our bounds if we simply ignore the images given and psychologize the reality of hell. An ancient tradition of the Christian Church holds that because of the very nature of the resurrection, the sufferings of hell must include not only the awful pain of separation from God but corporeal suffering as well. Just as we will be judged in the body for deeds done in the body, we will also suffer in the body for deeds done in the body. God takes our bodily nature seriously both before and after death.

Another question about hell is whether it is indeed of eternal duration. The "scandal" of hell's eternity has led men to speculate that perhaps one day God will pardon those in hell and that they, along with the fallen angels and Satan, will eventually be reconciled to God. Such efforts to "demythologize" hell — or even ignore it completely — are becoming more common today both on the theological and popular levels.

Nowhere does Scripture indicate that this might be the case; it clearly states quite the contrary. The Christian Church has always condemned this attempt by the fallen mind to recast revelation in a way more pleasing to fallen man. The existence of hell and its eternal duration have been taught and affirmed as certain revelation throughout the centuries.[7]

---

[7] The Council of Constantinople in 543 explicitly rejected as unscriptural the notion that there will be an end to hell or an eventual recon-

One last question about eternal condemnation: Is it probable that those who have rejected Christ will be offered an opportunity for repentance and faith at the time of death or after death? All that can be said in this regard is that dying seems to be a time when faith is tested rather than suddenly given. Although deathbed conversions certainly happen, Scripture indicates that, in general, death is the moment of summons to judgment on the basis of a life's choices and decisions, and not primarily a "last chance". It seems fairly clear that if one is not ready before the moment of crisis, it is presumptuous to plan on "preparing" at the last minute (Mt 25:1–13; Jn 9:4).

In conjunction with the judgment, Satan, death, the rebellious angels, and rebellious humanity are all finally banished from the kingdom, undergo the "second death", and are condemned to eternal torment in the lake of fire (Rev 20:10–15). Those who have responded to God's offer of salvation enter into fullness of life: "Inherit the kingdom prepared for you from the creation of the world" (Mt 25:34).

---

ciliation of its inhabitants. The early creeds of the Church, the Fourth Lateran Council, and the Councils of Lyons, Florence, and Trent all reaffirmed the traditional teaching.

Under the leadership of John Paul II, the Catholic Church has again reaffirmed these truths: "In fidelity to the New Testament and tradition, the church believes in the happiness of the just who will one day be with Christ.

"She believes that there will be eternal punishment for the sinner, who will be deprived of the sight of God, and that this punishment will have a repercussion on the whole being of the sinner" (*Certain Questions regarding Eschatology,* from the Congregation for the Doctrine of the Faith, issued May 17, 1979, with the approval of Pope John Paul II).

Heaven is variously described in Scripture.[8] It is eternal life (Mt 25:46), "glory beyond compare" (2 Cor 4:17), a place in which the redeemed participate in the life of God in glorified, immortal, incorruptible bodies (1 Cor 15:35–55). It is "dwelling in the heavens" (2 Cor 5:1), "the city of the living God", which is filled with "angels in festal garb" (Heb 12:22). Heaven is "the new Jerusalem, the holy city", part of "a new heaven, a new earth" (Rev 21:1–4, 10–11; 2 Pet 3:13).

Perhaps the passage from Revelation says it best:

Then I saw new heavens and a new earth. The former heavens and the former earth had passed away, and the sea was no longer. I also saw a new Jerusalem, the holy city, coming down out of heaven from God, beautiful as a bride prepared to meet her husband. I heard a loud voice from the throne cry out: "This is God's dwelling among men. He shall dwell with them and they shall be his people and he shall be their God who is always with them. He shall wipe every tear from their eyes, and there shall be no more death or mourning, crying out or pain, for the former world has passed away" (Rev 21:1–4).

[8] CCC 1023–29.

EIGHT

Are God's Ways Fair?

Today when the truth of judgment is spoken, certain questions and objections are often posed. Let us briefly consider them here before concluding our treatment of the topic.

Is God Fair in His Judgments?

"Modern man" protests that a God who would allow people to be damned is unfair. Since God is love, many argue, the notions of punishment and hell must either be Old Testament leftovers or first-century cultural superstitions that are not really part of the revelation of Scripture.

This line of reasoning has a number of problems. First, accepting the parts of scriptural teaching that suit us and rejecting others is dangerous. If the revelatory status of the New Testament's clear and repeated teaching about hell and punishment is regarded as questionable, then its clear and repeated teaching about God's love should be equally suspect. On what basis do we accept or reject New Testament teaching? If we approach Scripture on the basis of what modern man finds appealing or credible or fair

—using his judgments as the criteria—we are, in effect, doing away with Scripture as the word of God. This, of course, is what many have done. As a result, some modern Scripture scholarship finds itself in the uncomfortable position of picking and choosing what are "really" the reliable parts of Scripture, but with no reliable criteria to guide the choice. It is far better to determine the intention of the scriptural teaching, submit to it, and form our own standards of judgments by it.

Indeed, Scripture itself teaches that the proper way to approach Scripture is to seek to be instructed and formed by the word of God, not to try to instruct and form it according to modern prejudices. The rebellion of fallen mankind against God is manifest, not just in the works of the fallen body, but also in the works of the fallen mind. One of these works is to exalt the understanding and mind of man over the understanding and mind of God and to sit in judgment over what God has decreed and spoken. This, of course, is nothing other than sin. The fact that this is a common way of approaching God and his word today does not make it any less sinful.

While at college, I was impressed by a statement of the French existentialist philosopher Camus: "I can't believe in a God who would allow innocent children to suffer." Sentiments like this are common today. However, now that I more clearly understand the fundamental situation of man before God, such a statement strikes me as blasphemous—not at all brave, courageous, or worthy of admiration. For mankind to describe the kind of God he's willing to believe in—namely, one who would match his impoverished, limited notion of justice—is the height of folly. It reveals a total incomprehension of who God is and who man is. It assumes that man's "natural" understanding of the universe, unilluminated by revelation from God, is adequate. The truth is quite the opposite: man's understanding of reality is partial and often twisted and perverted.

Man cannot form judgments about what is "fair" and "just" without a certain spiritual framework. He must first acknowledge God's work in the person and mission of Christ and understand the truths of redemption, the Lord's coming, and the resurrection and judgment of mankind. Any other perspective is folly.

Scripture does not tell us all we would like to know; it tells us what we *need* to know. What it already tells us, and what we need to know, is enough to silence the most impassioned of human protest. Scripture reveals to us the presence of God in our midst—a mystery of such truth, love, and justice that only human silence and submission are appropriate. Would that Camus had recognized this, as Job did:

> "Who is this that obscures divine plans with words of ignorance? . . . Would you condemn me that you may be justified? . . ." Then Job answered the Lord and said: "I know that you can do all things, and that no purpose of yours can be hindered. I have dealt with great things that I do not understand; things too wonderful for me, which I cannot know. I had heard of you by word of mouth, but now my eye has seen you. Therefore I disown what I have said, and repent in dust and ashes" (Job 38:2; 40:8; 42:1–6).

Job perceived the greatness and majesty of God, his utter superiority to men. With that perception, Job realized that he was in no position to demand answers from God; the initiative lay with God, and his own part was to be instructed.

Job's example remains relevant for us today. God has told us everything we need to know to be saved. When some of our questions go unanswered, we do not "demand" answers. They remain the prerogative and initiative of God, and our appropriate stance can only be a reverential silence. This is obviously not to say that the theological task to seek greater understanding is not important or fruitful but rather that, even in these important efforts at faith seeking understanding, reverence before the greatness of the mystery is essential.

When we try to wrap the powers of our weak human minds around the immensity of such realities as eternity, judgment, heaven and hell, justice and mercy, we can receive only so much light. Having encountered God, our task is then to acknowledge what we know to be true, even without knowing *all* that is true:

> The law of the Lord is perfect,
>   refreshing the soul;
> The decree of the Lord is trustworthy,
>   giving wisdom to the simple.
> The precepts of the Lord are right,
>   rejoicing the heart;
> The command of the Lord is clear,
>   enlightening the eye.
>
>   (Ps 19:8–9)

Confronted with the reality of an unending hell, our minds sometimes strain to ask: "If man can be damned, why did God make us with a freedom that gave us such a capability?" The standard answer, and a good one, is that he gave us freedom because he wanted to confer immense dignity on us by creating us in his image. God gave us the freedom to choose, to join him or not to join him, to accept his invitation or to reject it — even though our choice would have eternal consequences. In this way, we will form a kingdom of free subjects who have chosen to be with God, not beings who have been coerced into doing the right thing.

At the same time, we must always add that if God created man as he did, then it must have been the perfect way of going about it, the perfectly right means of giving him freedom, the perfect risk to run, even at the expense of rejection and damnation. His ways are perfect. He is God. He is not only fair, he is the standard of fairness; he is not only love, he is the standard of love; he is not only just, he is the standard of justice. All his words will come to pass; all he wills is to be accomplished.

Is Man Truly Responsible for His Actions?

With the development of depth psychology, a tendency already present in modern thought became predominant: namely, the belief that man is so much a product of forces beyond his control that he is truly responsible for his actions only in a rather minimal way. Man is seen as the product of "economic laws of history", social and cultural forces, and drives and desires of his own psyche, such as sex and hostility and the will to power. These attitudes have even influenced God's people and have deeply affected prevailing understandings of sin in the Church in recent years. Many moral theologians have so restricted the possibility of freely choosing to do serious wrong that serious sin and hell seem to be distant possibilities, existing mainly in the realm of memories rather than among the present truths that shape our lives and govern our actions. Large segments within the Church today are taking a very permissive approach toward sin. Christians are being led to believe that the objective standards of God, as contained in the Scriptures and taught by the Christian Church across the centuries, might not really be applicable in their own life situations or, if they are applicable, that their violation would incur no blame.[1]

Scripture's view of man's responsibility for his actions is quite different from that of thinkers influenced by modern Marxist, behaviorist, and Freudian theories. In all of its relevant parts and in its entirety, Scripture clearly holds that man is responsible before God for his actions and that he will be judged accordingly. Scripture, without denying their possible relevance, does not focus on determining the degree to which mitigating circumstances (unfortunate childhood experiences, poverty, and so on) or other people (parents, "society") may have contributed to a person's wrong behavior, thereby lessening his guilt. Scripture

---

[1] This situation has led one distinguished Christian philosopher to write an article entitled "Do Moral Theologians Corrupt Youth?", answering his question in the affirmative. (Ralph McInerny, "Do Moral Theologians Corrupt Youth?" [*New Covenant*, November 1979, 4–7.])

quite clearly shows that God expects man to obey the law
he has placed within him and the law he has revealed to
him, availing himself of the help provided in and through
his Son and his body, the Christian people. Not to obey
God in a serious matter—these are listed clearly in Scripture, and we have already considered them—puts one in
danger of judgment. Even when Scripture does consider
what we might call mitigating circumstances, it does not
give modern man much comfort: ignorance of God's will
does not eliminate punishment, even though it may lessen
it. "The slave who knew his master's wishes but did not
prepare to fulfill them will get a severe beating, whereas
the one who did not know them and who nonetheless de-
served to be flogged will get off with fewer stripes. More
will be asked of a man to whom more has been entrusted"
(Lk 12:47–48).

How God may judge a particular case of allegedly "mitigating circumstances" is not our place to say, just as it
is not ours to determine who will be damned and who
will be saved. God makes the judgments. At the same
time, a Christian teacher would be extremely remiss in his
duty if he did not clearly state the overall picture given
in Scripture: God holds man responsible for his actions,
and the prospect of damnation for those who violate his
commands is very real.

Have They Really Heard the Gospel?

Since Scripture insists that men who hear the gospel and
reject it are liable to damnation, various questions have

been raised concerning the manner in which the gospel is presented. What constitutes an effective communication of the gospel? When can we say that someone has truly heard it? Sometimes this question is raised in an honest concern for effective evangelism. Other times it stems from the repugnance of modern man regarding clear scriptural statements about the consequences of rejecting the gospel and from his desire to rule out the possibility that he could be punished.

Is there anything in Scripture that can throw light on this question? Two passages can help us here. The first is in the Letter to the Romans, where Paul is considering what in the preaching of the gospel brings people to faith. In the course of Paul's teaching, he asks whether the Jews of his and Jesus' generation have truly heard the gospel, given the fact that most of them apparently rejected it. His answer is unequivocal: "Certainly they have heard."

> I ask you, have they not heard? Certainly they have, for "their voice has sounded over the whole earth, and their words to the limits of the world." I put the question again, did Israel really not understand? First of all, Moses says, "I will make you jealous of those who are not even a nation; with a senseless nation I will make you angry." Then Isaiah says boldly, "I was found by those who were not seeking me; to those who were not looking for me I revealed myself." But of Israel he says, "All day long I stretched out my hand to an unbelieving and contentious people" (Rom 10:18–21).

Paul obviously thinks the word has been adequately proclaimed to the Jews as a whole, who were at the time dispersed throughout the known world. He considers their rejection of it as yet another outbreak of the kind of unbelief and contentiousness that God severely punished and judged morally culpable in the Old Testament. It is not a question of their not having heard or understood.

Of course, this example does not immediately put us in a position to judge whether someone has really heard and understood the gospel in a given situation. But it should put us on guard against assuming too quickly that the presentation of the message of salvation is deficient. The massive rejection of Jesus by the Jews of his day and Paul's stands as sobering evidence that even masses of people can both hear and understand the gospel and yet reject it, to their own condemnation.

For our part we should make every effort to present the gospel adequately and not remain content with unnecessarily offensive or deficient presentations. We should, of course, make every effort to ensure that our lives, actions, and relationships reflect the truth of the gospel well. But we should not delude ourselves into thinking that we need an advanced academic degree in communications to communicate the gospel adequately; nor do our lives have to be perfectly transformed before others can truly hear and understand. The awe-inspiring truth is that people — and large numbers of them — can both hear and understand and yet reject.

Another passage that throws light on this question is the ending of the story of Dives and Lazarus. Dives finally pleads that Lazarus be allowed to go to the rich man's brothers to prevent their ending up in hell:

> Abraham answered, "They have Moses and the prophets. Let them hear them." "No, Father Abraham", replied the rich man. "But if someone would only go to them from the dead, then they would repent." Abraham said to him, "If they do not listen to Moses and the prophets, they will not be convinced even if one should rise from the dead" (Lk 16:27–31).

Having a clear grasp on the sobering reality that men can both hear and understand, yet reject, is imperative if we are to conduct ourselves properly as individuals and as a Christian Church in the modern world. If we fail to face up to the genuine anti-Christian, anti-Church, anti-God hostility that is at the root of many of the most "progressive" modern trends and developments, we run the risk of taking a sentimental, foolish approach to them. One Catholic historian pointed out that many Christians find it impossible to recognize the depth and strength of anti-Christian feeling in the Western world, and they console themselves that where it does exist, it is based upon disappointment with Christians who do not live up to their beliefs. In fact, however, the Church is hated not primarily because her members fall short of her teachings but precisely because she insists on being what she is supposed to be. She speaks of God, of eternity, or right and wrong. It is the Church's fidelities that are despised, not her infidelities.

Will Many Be Lost?

In trying to grasp and interpret properly what Scripture tells us about the reality of judgment, we may naturally wonder about the relative proportions of the saved to the damned. Sometimes we ask the question in order to determine how seriously to take the word of God and how much effort to expend in keeping and following it. Scripture's answer is sobering: We must take God's word very seriously and keep and follow it very closely, for "the invited are many, the elect are few" (Mt 22:14). Compared to the number who are invited into the kingdom — all men — relatively few accept the invitation. About this Jesus explicitly warns:

> Enter through the narrow gate. The gate that leads to damnation is wide, the road is clear, and many choose to travel it. But how narrow is the gate that leads to life, how rough the road, and how few there are who find it! (Mt 27:13–14).

Scripture indicates a final difficulty: the mass apostasy that will occur at the culmination of history in the events leading up to Jesus' return (2 Th 2:3). "Because of the increase of evil, the love of most will grow cold", and only "the man who holds out to the end . . . will see salvation" (Mt 24:12–13). Peter says:

> The season of judgment has begun, and begun with God's own household. If it begins this way with us, what must be the end for those who refuse obedience to the gospel of God? And if the just man is saved

only with difficulty, what is to become of the godless and the sinner? (1 Pet 4:17–18).

Scripture indicates that one does not enter the kingdom by drifting along with the prevailing culture or by doing what most men do. Christians need to break with what most men do and how most men live and think. We must choose to submit to Christ and live as members of his body, the Church, evaluating and understanding all of reality with the mind of Christ, in the light of eternity.

C. S. Lewis expressed the importance of living our lives with an "eternal perspective" quite strikingly:

It is a serious thing to live in a society of possible gods and goddesses, to remember that the dullest and most uninteresting person you talk to may one day be a creature which, if you saw it now, you would be tempted to worship, or else a horror and a corruption such as you now meet, if at all, only in a nightmare. All day long we are, in some degree, helping each other to one or the other of these destinations.[2]

---

[2] C. S. Lewis, *The Weight of Glory and Other Addresses* (Grand Rapids, Mich.: William B. Eerdmans, 1965), 14–15.

NINE

Is Jesus Coming Soon?

In both Catholic and Protestant circles there is quite a lot of attention being paid to what appears to be an upsurge of the action of God in the world. In Catholic circles a lot of this, although not all, is connected with the action of Mary as an agent of God, whether by reported apparitions, weeping icons, or reported locutions (interior communications). The thrust of many of these manifestations is an urgent call to conversion as preparation for an especially significant action of God in the near future that may involve a supernatural warning to the whole earth, special miracles, and perhaps an experience of chastisement and judgment.

As the twentieth century has unfolded and draws to a close, the number of purported appearances of Mary in countries throughout the world has mushroomed. In recent years there has been a veritable explosion in reports of Mary's prophetic intervention, whether it be through apparitions, visions, or locutions. By one recent count, there have been 232 reports of such events in thirty-two separate countries.[1]

[1] Fr. Michael Scanlan, "The Marian Movement", *New Covenant*, March 1993, 23.

The messages are strikingly similar: a time of chastisement is coming to the world; God is showing mercy in sending his Mother and offering time for repentance and conversion; prayer, holiness, love are keys to extending God's mercy to the world. While undoubtedly not all of these purported apparitions are on the same level of importance or validity as Guadalupe, Lourdes, or Fatima, there can be no question that something extraordinary is happening by way of divine warning. Mary continues in so many different ways to point to Jesus and tell us: Do whatever he tells you. The Father continues to tell the world in so many different ways, including through his handmaiden, Mary: This is my beloved Son in whom I am well pleased, listen to him. The Holy Spirit continues to speak through his servants, the prophets, and through Mary, Queen of Prophets.

Some believe that just as God used Mary in a special way to prepare for the First Coming of his Son, he is currently using Mary to prepare for the Second Coming of Jesus. In the early eighteenth century St. Louis de Montfort prophesied:

> It was through Mary that the salvation of the world was begun, and it is through Mary that it must be consummated.[2]

Could the tears of Mary, witnessed to in so many contemporary accounts, be a participation in the tears of Jesus as he wept over the city of Jerusalem, foreseeing its impending destruction? Is Jesus now weeping over the cities

[2] St. Louis de Montfort, *True Devotion to Mary* (Rockford, Ill.: Tan Publishers, 1985), II, 3, 49, p. 28.

of our world? Are we in danger of missing the hour of our visitation?

In Protestant circles this sense of the imminent action of God seems to be expressed in an upsurge in unusually powerful "revivals" with unusual manifestations of the Holy Spirit, a sense of imminent evangelistic breakthroughs, and a prophetic sense that we are about to see a great harvest of souls that will prepare the way for the return of the Lord.

There seems to be a growing sense in both Catholic and Protestant circles that at the very least the next several years are going to be of great spiritual significance, either because of the nearness of Jesus' return or because of a significant spiritual turning point that will improve the prospects of the spread of Christianity in the world.

Pope John Paul II in his repeated calls to prepare for the year 2000 and the new millennium has emphasized the fact that the Great Jubilee of the birth of the Lord that he has declared for the year 2000 is to be not just a *pro forma* ritualistic celebration but a genuine encounter with God and a manifestation of his grace to the world. He often has called us to live the years leading to the year 2000 as a "new advent" explicitly linking the action of God that he expects to be made manifest in the Great Jubilee to the themes of the coming of Christ contained in the Church's understanding of Advent. He has even spoken of preparation for the year 2000 as "a hermeneutical key of my Pontificate".[3] In what can only be called a prophetic utterance, he has frequently spoken of: "*that*

[3] John Paul II, *On Preparation for the Jubilee of the Year 2000 (Tertio Millennio Adveniente)*, 23.

new springtime of Christian life which will be revealed by the Great Jubilee, if Christians are docile to the action of the Holy Spirit".[4] At another point he declared: "As the third millennium of the redemption draws near, God is preparing a great springtime for Christianity, and we can already see its first signs."[5]

What might some of these signs be?

The Brownsville Assembly of God in Pensacola, Florida, is experiencing a powerful visitation from God with more than ninety thousand committing their lives to Christ in the last two years.

More than twenty million have visited Medjugorje in the sixteen years that Mary is reported to have been appearing there, and there have been innumerable reports of many, many conversions and healings. The visionaries there have reported that Mary has told them that more grace is being poured out on the world today than ever before, and that the reason Satan is so active today is that he knows his time is now short.

In recent years stadiums full of men across the United States have echoed with the sounds of repentance, commitment, and praise. In 1996 alone, more than twenty-four stadiums full of more than a million men have committed themselves to be Promise Keepers. This is an extraordinary development given the frequent lack of male involvement in many of the churches.

By early 1997 more than one million people had visited the Toronto Airport church, which is the scene of

[4] Ibid., 18.
[5] John Paul II, *Mission of the Redeemer*, 3, 86.

an ongoing revival. Over twenty thousand pastors and other Christian leaders have visited, and many have experienced profound renewal and refreshment and deeper conversion. Planeloads of people from around the world have come, many from England, where more than seven thousand churches have been significantly impacted by this renewal.

And a priest we work with in Uganda[6] has just written to say:

> I wish I could show to each one of you some of the photos I have received of what's happening in some of the parishes in the Hoima Diocese. In Huhoro there are hundreds of people who come together every Wednesday; in Mugalike it is close to 2000 who cram the church every Thursday. And week after week there are fresh reports about extraordinary healings: the withered hand of a man gets restored; a paralyzed woman who for several weeks has been carried to Prayer Meetings suddenly during a time of praise and worship jumps up and is well; only last week a boy of 15, crippled from birth who had never walked, gets up and walks. The leadership is so new in these two parishes that only two people have ever made a Life in the Spirit Seminar. Perhaps the biggest miracle is that the priests and the Bishops support

[6] If anyone is interested in following the work of Renewal Ministries, the Catholic mission organization that I serve as president, they can request a free subscription to our monthly newsletter by writing to: Renewal Ministries, P.O. Box 7712, Ann Arbor, Michigan, 48103; or in Canada, Renewal Ministries, P.O. Box 160, Etobicoke, Ontario, M9C4V2.

this move of the Spirit. This revival is now spreading to additional parishes!

A short time later we received a report from a priest in a rural area of Uganda that over six thousand people showed up for a Life in the Spirit Seminar that he had announced in his parish.

In India a group of priests is now leading a revival that is quite impressive. What started as a small prayer group in Potta, southern India, has now become the world's largest retreat center, where twelve to fifteen thousand people attend a live-in week-long retreat, every week of the year. Recently, at a special one-week retreat for teenagers, eighteen thousand attended. Besides the live-in retreat each week, there are also daily retreats for anyone who is interested. These are attended by three to five thousand people each weekday, swelling to from thirty to fifty thousand on Saturdays. One of the most hopeful signs is that tens of thousands of Hindus are being converted to Christ, many because of the signs and wonders they see being performed in the name of Jesus.

Could we be seeing the emergence of the prophets and apostles of the new evangelization that John Paul II called for when he said: "Dear brothers, the new evangelization awaits its prophets and apostles."[7] Perhaps these prophets and apostles will be those prophesied by St. Louis de Montfort, in the eighteenth century, who will appear in

---

[7] Pope John Paul II, "Lights and Shadows Mark the Life of the Church in Portugal", *L'Osservatore Romano*, English language ed., December 9, 1992, 3.

as they cried when He was in the body, "We know Thee Who Thou art, the Holy One of God," and "Ah, what have I in common with Thee, Thou Son of God? I implore Thee, torment me not" (cf. Lk 4:34 and Mk 5:7).

Both from the confession of the evil spirits and from the daily witness of His works, it is manifest, then, and let none presume to doubt it, that the Saviour has raised His own body, and that He is the very Son of God, having His being from God as from a Father, Whose Word and Wisdom and Whose Power He is. He it is Who in these latter days assumed a body for the salvation of us all, and taught the world concerning the Father. He it is Who has destroyed death and freely graced us all with incorruption through the promise of the resurrection, having raised His own body as its first-fruits, and displayed it by the sign of the cross as the monument to His victory over death and its corruption.

§48 These things which we have said are no mere words: they are attested by actual experience. Anyone who likes may see the proof of glory in the virgins of Christ, and in the young men who practice chastity as part of their religion, and in the assurance of immortality in so great and glad a company of martyrs. Anyone, too, may put what we have said to the proof of experience in another way. In the very presence of the fraud of daemons and the imposture of the oracles and the wonders of magic, let him use the sign of the cross which they all mock at, and but speak the Name of Christ, and he shall see how through Him daemons are routed, oracles cease, and all magic and witchcraft confounded.

Who, then, is this Christ and how great is He, Who by His Name and presence overshadows and confounds all things on every side, Who alone is strong against all and has filled the whole world with His teaching?

Why the Jews Should Believe

§40 What more is there for their Expected One to do when he comes? To call the heathen? But they are called already. To put an end to prophet and king and vision? But this too has already happened. To expose the God-denyingness of idols? It is already exposed and condemned. Or to destroy death? It is already destroyed. What then has not come to pass that the Christ must do? What is there left out or unfulfilled that the Jews should disbelieve so light-heartedly? The plain fact is, as I say, that there is no longer any king or prophet nor Jerusalem nor sacrifice nor vision among them; yet the whole earth is filled with the knowledge of God, and the Gentiles, forsaking atheism, are now taking refuge with the God of Abraham through the Word, our Lord Jesus Christ.

Why the Gentiles Should Believe

§47 As to Greek wisdom, however, and the philosophers' noisy talk, I really think no one requires argument from us; for the amazing fact is patent to all that, for all that they have written so much, the Greeks failed to convince even a few from their own neighbourhood in regard to immortality and the virtuous ordering of life. Christ alone, using common speech and through the agency of men not clever with their tongues, has convinced whole assemblies of people all the world over to despise death, and to take heed to the things that do not die, to look past the things of time and gaze on things eternal, to think nothing of earthly glory and to aspire only to immortality.

§50 Many before Him have been kings and tyrants of the earth, history tells also of many among the Chaldaeans and Egyptians and Indians who were wise men and magicians. But which of those, I do not say after his death, but while yet in this life, was ever able so far to prevail as to fill the whole world with his teaching and retrieve so great a multitude from the craven fear of idols, as our Saviour has won over from idols to Himself? The Greek philosophers have compiled many works with persuasiveness and much skill in words; but what fruit have they to show for this such as has the cross of Christ? Their wise thoughts were persuasive enough until they died; yet even in their life-time their seeming influence was counter-balanced by their rivalry with one another, for they were a jealous company and declaimed against each other. But the Word of God, by strangest paradox, teaching in meaner language, has put the choicest sophists in the shade, and by confounding their teachings and drawing all men to Himself He has filled His own assemblies. Moreover, and this is the marvelous thing, by going down as Man to death He has confounded all the sounding utterances of the wise men about the idols. For whose death ever drove out daemons, or whose death did ever daemons fear, save that of Christ? For where the Saviour is named, there every daemon is driven out. Again, who has ever so rid men of their natural passions that fornicators become chaste and murderers no longer wield the sword and those who formerly were craven cowards boldly play the man? In a word, what persuaded the barbarians and heathen folk in every place to drop their madness and give heed to peace, save the faith of Christ and the sign of the cross? What other things have given men such certain faith in immortality as have the cross of Christ and the resurrection of His body? The Greeks told all sorts of false tales, but they never pretend that their idols rose again from death: indeed it never entered their heads that a body could exist again after death at all. And one would be particularly ready to listen to them on this point, because by these opinions they have exposed the weakness of their own idolatry, at the same time yielding to Christ the possibility of bodily resurrection, so that by that means He might be recognized by all as Son of God.

The Social Effect of the Gospel

§51 Again, who among men, either after his death or while yet living, taught about virginity and did not account this virtue impossible for human beings? But Christ our Saviour and King of all has so prevailed with His teaching on this subject that even children not yet of lawful age promise that virginity which transcends the law. And who among men has ever been able to penetrate even to Scythians and Ethiopians, or Parthians or Armenians or those who are said to live beyond Hyrcania, or even the Egyptians and Chaldaeans, people who give heed to magic and are more than naturally enslaved by the fear of daemons and savage in their habits, and to preach at all about virtue and self-control and against the worshipping of idols, as has the Lord of all, the Power of God, our Lord Jesus Christ? Yet He not only preached through His own disciples, but also wrought so persuasively on men's understanding that, laying aside their savage habits and forsaking the worship of their ancestral gods, they learnt to know Him and through Him to worship the Father. While they were yet idolaters, the Greeks and Barbarians were always at war with each other, and were even cruel to their own kith and kin. Nobody could travel by land or sea at all unless he was armed with swords, because of their irreconcilable quarrels with each other. Indeed, the whole course of their life was carried on with the weapons, and the sword with them replaced the staff and was the mainstay of all aid. All this time, as I said before, they were serving idols and offering sacrifices to daemons, and for all the superstitious awe that accompanied this idol worship, nothing could wean them from that warlike spirit. But, strange to relate, since they came over to the school of Christ, as men moved with real compunction they have laid aside their murderous cruelty and are war-minded no more. On the contrary, all is peace among them and nothing remains save desire for friendship.

§52 Who, then, is He Who has done these things and has united in peace those who hated each other, save the beloved Son of the Father, the common Saviour of all, Jesus Christ, who by His own love underwent all things for our salvation? Even from the beginning, moreover, this peace that He was to administer was foretold, for Scripture says, "They shall beat their swords into ploughshares and their spears into sickles, and nation shall not take sword against nation, neither shall they learn any more to wage war" (Is 2:4). Nor is this by any means incredible. The barbarians of the present day are naturally savage in their habits, and as long as they sacrifice to their idols they rage furiously against each other and cannot bear to be a single hour without weapons. But when they hear the teaching of Christ, forthwith they turn from fighting to farming, and instead of arming themselves with swords extend their hands in prayer. In a word, instead of fighting each other, they take up arms against the devil and the daemons, and overcome them by their self-command and integrity of soul. These facts are proof of the Godhead of the Saviour, for He has taught men what they could never learn among idols. It is also no small exposure of the weakness and nothingness of daemons and idols, for it was because they knew their own weakness that the daemons were always setting men to fight each other, fearing lest, if they ceased from mutual strife, they would turn to attack the daemons themselves. For in truth the disciples of Christ instead of fighting each other, stand arrayed against daemons by their habits and virtuous actions, and chase them away and mock at their captain the devil. Even in youth they are chaste, they endure in times of testing and persevere in toils. When they are insulted, they are patient, when robbed they make light of it, and, marvelous to relate, they make light even of death itself, and become martyrs of Christ.

§53 And here is another proof of the Godhead of the Saviour, which is indeed utterly amazing. What mere man or magician or tyrant or king was ever able by himself to do so much? Did anyone ever fight against the whole system of idol-worship and the whole host of daemons and all magic and all the wisdom of the Greeks, at a time when all of these were strong and flourishing and taking everybody in, as did our Lord, the very Word of God? Yet He is even now invisibly exposing every man's error, and single-handed is carrying off all men from them all, so that those who used to worship idols now tread them under foot, reputed magicians burn their books and the wise prefer to all studies the interpretation of the gospels. They are deserting those whom formerly they worshipped, they worship and confess as Christ and God Him Whom they used to ridicule as crucified. Their so-called gods are routed by the sign of the cross, and the crucified Saviour is proclaimed in all the world as God and Son of God. Moreover, the gods worshipped among the Greeks are now falling into disrepute among them on account of the disgraceful things they did, for those who receive the teaching of Christ are more chaste in life than they.

§55 Since the Saviour's advent in our midst, not only does idolatry no longer increase, but it is getting less and gradually ceasing to be. Similarly, not only does the wisdom of the Greeks no longer make any progress, but that which used to be is disappearing. And daemons, so far from continuing to impose on people by their deceits and oracle-givings and sorceries, are routed by the sign of the cross if they so much as try. On the other hand, while idolatry and everything else that opposes the faith of Christ is daily dwindling and weakening and falling, see, the Saviour's teaching is increasing everywhere! Worship, then, the Saviour "Who is above all" and mighty, even God the Word, and condemn those who are being defeated and made to disappear by Him.

The Scripture and the Second Coming

§56 Here, then, Macarius, is our offering to you who love Christ, a brief statement of the faith of Christ and of the manifestation of His Godhead to us. This will give you a beginning, and you must go on to prove its truth by the study of the Scriptures. They were written and inspired by God; and we, who have learned from inspired teachers who read the Scriptures and became martyrs for the Godhead of Christ, make further contribution to your eagerness to learn. From the Scriptures you will learn also of His second manifestation to us, glorious and divine indeed, when He shall come not in lowliness but in His proper glory, no longer in humiliation but in majesty, no longer to suffer but to bestow on us all the fruit of His cross — the resurrection and incorruptibility. No longer will He then be judged, but rather will Himself be Judge, judging each and all according to their deeds done in the body, whether good or ill. Then for the good is laid up the heavenly kingdom, but for those that practice evil outer darkness and the eternal fire. So also the Lord Himself says, "I say unto you, hereafter ye shall see the Son of Man seated on the right hand of power, coming on the clouds of heaven in the glory of the Father" (Mt 14:64). For that Day we have one of His own sayings to prepare us, "Get ready and watch, for ye know not the hour in which He cometh" (Mt 24:42). And blessed Paul says, "We must all stand before the judgment seat of Christ, that each one may receive according as he practised in the body, whether good or ill" (2 Cor 5:10).

§57 But for the searching and right understanding of the Scriptures there is need of a good life and a pure soul, and for Christian virtue to guide the mind to grasp, so far as human nature can, the truth concerning God the Word. One cannot possibly understand the teaching of the saints unless one has a pure mind and is trying to imitate their life. Anyone who wants to look at sunlight naturally wipes his eye clear first, in order to make, at any rate, some approximation to the purity of that on which he looks; and a person wishing to see a city or country goes to the place in order to do so. Similarly, anyone who wishes to understand the mind of the sacred writers must first cleanse his own life, and approach the saints by copying their deeds. Thus united to them in the fellowship of life, he will both understand the things revealed to them by God and thenceforth escaping the peril that threatens sinners in the judgment, will receive that which is laid up for the saints in the kingdom of heaven. Of that reward it is written: "Eye hath not seen nor ear heard, neither hath entered into the heart of man the things that God has prepared" (1 Cor 2:9) for them that live a godly life and love the God and Father in Christ Jesus our Lord, through Whom and with Whom be to the Father Himself, with the Son Himself, in the Holy Spirit, honour and might and glory to ages of ages. Amen.